The Aims of Higher Education

D1566153

The Aims of Higher Education

Problems of Morality and Justice

Edited by

HARRY BRIGHOUSE

MICHAEL MCPHERSON

The University of Chicago Press
Chicago and London

Harry Brighouse is professor of philosophy at the University of Wisconsin–Madison. He is the author or coauthor of several books, including *On Education*, and most recently, *Family Values: The Ethics of Parent-Child Relationships*. **Michael McPherson** is president of the Spencer Foundation and was previously the president of Macalester College in St. Paul. He is coauthor or editor of several books, including *Economic Analysis, Moral Philosophy, and Public Policy*.

The University of Chicago Press, Chicago 60637
The University of Chicago Press, Ltd., London
© 2015 by The University of Chicago.
All rights reserved. Published 2015.
Printed in the United States of America

24 23 22 21 20 19 18 17 16 15   1 2 3 4 5

ISBN-13: 978-0-226-25934-5 (cloth)
ISBN-13: 978-0-226-25948-2 (paper)
ISBN-13: 978-0-226-25951-2 (e-book)
DOI: 10.7208/chicago/9780226259512.001.0001

A version of chapter 2, by Amy Gutmann, appeared under the title "What It's Worth: The Value of a University Education" in the special issue of *Carnegie Reporter* 7, no. 3 (Winter 2014).

Library of Congress Cataloging-in-Publication Data

The aims of higher education : problems of morality and justice / edited by Harry Brighouse and Michael McPherson.
        pages cm
    Includes bibliographical references and index.
    ISBN 978-0-226-25934-5 (cloth : alk. paper) — ISBN 978-0-226-25948-2 (pbk. : alk. paper) — ISBN 978-0-226-25951-2 (e-book) 1. Education, Higher—Moral and ethical aspects. 2. Education, Higher—Aims and objectives. I. Brighouse, Harry. II. McPherson, Michael S.
    LB2324.A39 2015
    378.001—dc23
                            2014041929

♾ This paper meets the requirements of ANSI/NISO Z39.48-1992 (Permanence of Paper).

CONTENTS

ONE

Introduction:
Problems of Morality and Justice
in Higher Education

HARRY BRIGHOUSE AND MICHAEL MCPHERSON

About 60 percent of Americans have higher education, and some 40 percent graduate with some sort of post–high school degree. Graduating from college has a significant effect on one's lifetime earnings, on the kind of work one is able to perform, and on one's health and longevity. It is a prerequisite for many lucrative careers, and graduating from a more selective college often gives someone an advantage over a competitor from a less selective one in professional labor markets. In other words, access to higher education is an important factor in the competition for the benefits our society distributes unequally. But higher education is also a factor in creating those benefits. Education makes people more productive economically and more capable socially, and it enables them to use their leisure time in more fulfilling ways.

College is not just good for the income and life prospects of graduates. They also get to enjoy the experience of being in college itself—a time that is widely regarded as one of self-exploration in which they can learn more about their own talents and inclinations and how these fit into the wider world. Furthermore, students can accumulate knowledge and understanding of the world and develop their talents. In other words, they learn. This is why, in addition to advantaging graduates in labor-market competition, higher education also makes them more productive: it contributes to the creation of the pool of unequally distributed benefits that graduates are better placed to win.

Most students do not attend highly selective colleges: they go to colleges for which the only qualification is a high school diploma or a GED. But highly selective colleges play a crucial role in the formation of elites in our society. They educate the young people who will later form large proportions of lawmakers, businessmen and businesswomen, education and public sector leaders, and judges at the state, national, and even international levels, as well as most other high-status professionals.

So it is natural that highly selective higher education should be the focus of a great deal of public policy and scholarly debate. What role should the liberal arts have in a college education? Should colleges orient themselves to the educational demands of the business sector? What is the role of highly selective colleges in the public sphere? To what extent should they be subsidized, either directly or indirectly, by the public? Should they simply teach students skills and academic knowledge, or should they play a role in shaping character, and if so, to what end? Should highly selective colleges' admissions practices give an edge to racial minorities, legacies, or poor students? How much should the public purse subsidize disadvantaged students attending such institutions?

These debates are fundamentally about values, and we believe that moral and political philosophers can contribute in useful ways. Deciding exactly which policies and practices we should adopt demands careful attention to the empirical evidence supplied by social science. It also requires thinking about what we ought to value—about questions of distributive justice and of what constitutes a valuable education. Philosophers are trained to identify value considerations in great detail—to specify them with just a little more precision than would ever be needed for practical purposes. In our experiences, disagreements about policy and practice often proceed with minimal attention to the values assumed on either side. However, all sides can benefit from more clarity about which moral values are in play.

We can crudely divide the moral issues concerning higher education into three overlapping categories. The first concerns what students should learn. Should college prepare students to be maximally productive, economically speaking? Should it focus on developing citizens with powerful deliberative capacities and the inclination to use them for the public good? Should it challenge the opinions and religious and cultural assumptions students bring with them? Should it shape students' views about what is valuable in life and valuable to learn? Or should it respond to their preferences and allow them to shape their own values? Should it do all or just some of these things? Should different colleges aim at different balances?

The second category concerns who should attend college. Should college be just for the few elite who will occupy privileged positions in our society? Should college be a prerequisite for all professions? Should parental income and wealth influence who goes to which college, and whether somebody goes at all? Should everybody, or nearly everybody, go to college, just as everybody goes to high school? Should colleges attend to diversity considerations in regulating access? Should we have some institutions that are much more selective than others?

The third category concerns the relationship between universities and the wider world. Should universities pursue commercially sponsored research? Who should own the knowledge that the universities produce? Should universities enjoy the benefits of tax-exempt status? Should they be involved in running public services, such as hospitals and schools? When and how should interested parties outside universities have a say in what is taught, and in what ways?

We charged the authors of the chapters in this volume with addressing some of these fundamental questions about the values underlying debates about higher education and asked them to do so in ways that would be interesting and accessible to other philosophers, scholars, policy makers, administrators, students, and members of the general public who are engaged in the debates. We invited contributors who we were confident had an informed interest in the selective and very selective colleges segment of higher education and who had a record of producing distinguished philosophical work. All have been students and teachers, and several either have been or currently are leaders and administrators. We did not assign a question to each contributor, but instead gave them free rein to address the questions that most interested them. Their contributions mostly engage with questions that clearly arise in the segment of higher education they inhabit. We did not ask the authors to attempt to work out the extent or ways in which their conclusions might apply to other segments of higher education—nonselective colleges, community colleges, or for-profit institutions. This is not because we believe those segments are less important, nor because we believe that the conclusions they draw do not apply more widely. It is because we do believe that exploring the commonalities of and differences between the diverse institutions of higher education is a substantial intellectual task that would, in this context, distract from the main purpose. Some of our readers work in the other segments or at least know them well and are better qualified than we or the contributors to judge what bearing these chapters have on those systems and institutions. In fact, we hope that some of our readers will be prompted by this volume to take on that task.

None of the chapters focuses exclusively on questions that fall just within one category, because questions within each category bear on questions in the other categories. For example, how the university should relate to the wider society bears on what students should learn, which in turn bears on who should attend college. The volume opens with a contribution bearing on all three categories of question by Amy Gutmann, an eminent political theorist whose book *Democratic Education* (1987) shaped much subsequent moral and political theory applying to both K-12 and higher education, and who is now president of the University of Pennsylvania. Gutmann identifies three purposes of undergraduate education: *opportunity*—ensuring that students from the widest practical array of social backgrounds can enjoy education; *creative understanding*—ensuring that students become well prepared to think critically and practically about fundamental problems; and *contribution*—ensuring that the university and the students it produces are oriented to socially valuable production. Using data drawn from a study commissioned by her office, Gutmann presents a powerful argument that America's elite colleges are ready to expand access to a broader segment of society than they currently do, thus diversifying the elite that they play a key role in forming. Among highly qualified high school graduates, a much higher proportion of the most advantaged 20 percent attend elite colleges than of the next 60 percent.

Gutmann offers a defense of a kind of liberal arts education that is familiar in elite American colleges, arguing that it is essential for developing the creative understanding needed in order to contribute effectively to society. Christopher Bertram's chapter takes up a specific element of that liberal arts education, the humanities, and subjects two powerful defenses supporting the humanities in universities—that they are vital for the economy and that they are necessary to democracy—to powerful criticisms. His own argument for supporting the humanities—that they are a vital source of knowledge that cannot be obtained without the hermeneutic methods that the humanities have developed—fits well with Gutmann's defense of teaching the broader liberal arts, and with her conjecture that this teaching might sometimes be particularly important in the context of professional schools.

Kyla Ebels-Duggan's, Paul Weithman's, and Allen Buchanan's chapters in the volume complement one another. All concern the importance of developing certain character traits and skills in students. Ebels-Duggan offers an original characterization of personal autonomy as an educational goal. College teachers, especially in the humanities, like to think that they are developing their students' capacities for critical reflection by helping them to reflect on their received values and traditions and rationally to choose anew. This belief depends on a diagnosis of the problem that students are too wedded, and unreasoningly so, to some set of preexisting value commitments. By contrast, Ebels-Duggan observes that many students in elite institutions are in fact overconfident in their capacity to provide negative criticism. Students think they can show what is wrong with the arguments and claims of the thinkers they encounter. If this is the central problem, Ebels-Duggan argues, we need to teach students to be charitable and humble—charitable in their interpretation of the thinking and arguments of others, and humble in their stance toward their own critical faculties.[1] Developing their autonomy requires us to develop their character. Weithman's chapter similarly attends to the relationship between student and teacher, in the sense of developing an ideal that he calls "academic friendship." As an academic friend, the teacher plays a role in forming the students' characters, especially as it relates to the academic material that they study together. She does indeed seek to develop students' autonomy, as traditionally understood, but she also wants to introduce students to great intellectual achievements and to the complexity of the world in a way that fosters the right kind of response: humility in the face of those achievements and that complexity alongside some pride in having come to understand it better.

Both Ebels-Duggan and Weithman want to supplement autonomy as an educational aim with the development of certain moral virtues. Allen Buchanan's contribution tackles the problem that the world is so complex that none of us can possibly hope to have the knowledge we need to navigate it through our own exercise of reason. Nobody has the time, even if they have the cognitive capacities, to understand and investigate the complex science behind policy recommendations about climate change *and* the science and evidence concerning evolution *and* the social science behind claims about the desirability of gun control, school reform, and so on. On top of that fact, we are plagued with problems of what psychologists call "bounded rationality"—biases and norms that systematically derail us when we are making judgments about all sorts of matters, from statistical inferences to quality of musicianship. Education can play a key role in solving the expert/novice problem by helping students to identify which experts to trust. Buchanan identifies a series of particularly dangerous kinds of false beliefs—particularly those associated with cultural, national, and political identity—and suggests ways in which education can mitigate the likelihood of people holding these kinds of false beliefs.

The closing two chapters, by Erin I. Kelly and Lionel K. McPherson, focus on issues of distributive justice. Kelly's chapter homes in on what kind of justice is necessary for the university to deliver on its educational promise. She argues that for full success in producing students who can think critically, reason ethically, and contribute properly to the democratic process, selective colleges must have diverse populations of both students and faculty. When determining admissions, elite colleges should consider potential for both success and contribution. When hiring and promoting faculty, colleges should attend to the "social intelligence" of a candidate's scholarship. Rather than simply allowing disciplines to determine what research counts as excellent or valuable, colleges, because they have an educational mission, should make normative judgments about the significance of scholarship.

Lionel McPherson's chapter details the obligations elite colleges have to contribute to corrective justice. Colleges are institutions with identities that persist over time. Many elite campuses have been complicit in and benefited from racial injustice in the United States—through, for example, the GI Bill, which disproportionately benefited whites who were better able to access the resources of elite institutions and the social mobility they afforded. The injustices from which these institutions benefited have continuing unjust effects, so elite colleges have special obligations. McPherson specifically suggests a model that draws on the educational expertise of elite colleges: they should sponsor charter schools, which would deliberately select students in order to foster talented minority children and in that way provide a pathway to selective education, hence redressing the imbalance of social mobility in which these colleges have been complicit in the past.

The volume as a whole provides new and compelling normative perspectives, and arguments for these perspectives, on a range of issues that affect both policy and practice. We hope and, indeed, expect that readers of this volume who are engaged substantively with problems in higher education, whether as professors or administrators or in other ways, will find their own thinking and actions helpfully influenced by what they have read. We believe that the essays in this volume also embody important lessons for others, who themselves contemplate writing about normative problems in education, whether tackling their topics as social scientists, policy analysts, or moral philosophers. Good decision making in educational affairs and the fruitful analysis of social-science evidence are aided by careful reasoning about value issues, and philosophical analysis is enriched when it is connected to social-science evidence and practical questions—points that these chapters amply illustrate.

Notes

1. For another articulate defense of the same position, listen to the speech at the University of Minnesota's College of Liberal Arts 2012 commencement by hip-hop artist Dessa: https://www.youtube.com/watch?v=u38ue-XxHtw, starting at 17:20.

TWO

What Makes a University Education Worthwhile?

AMY GUTMANN

"A mind is a precious thing to waste," wrote Bill Gross, cofounder of the Pacific Investment Management Company, "so why are millions of America's students wasting theirs by going to college?"[1] In 2010 the cofounder of PayPal, Peter Thiel, announced that he would pay $100,000 each to twenty young people as an incentive for them to drop out of college and start a tech-based business. In May 2011 he chose twenty-two men and two women to receive this "skip-school scholarship."[2]

What gives the "skip-school scholarship" its shock value is the prevailing view that a university education is a valuable ticket to success. But instead of taking the worth of a university education for granted, many people are now asking the value-added question: do universities provide private and public benefits commensurate with their private and public costs?[3]

The most common way of answering this question is to tally up a university education's added income benefits to its graduates, subtract its added costs, and see whether the benefits exceed the costs. Some economists have done this quite well. The prevailing answer is that a college education has paid off for most graduates to date, and can be expected to do so in the future.[4]

What I want to convey in this essay, above all else, is that we cannot adequately answer the value-added question without first answering the more fundamental question about mission. What should universities aim to achieve for individuals and society?

It is reassuring to those who believe in the worth of a university education—especially in a high-unemployment, low-growth economy—to show that the average person with a college education earns a lot more over her lifetime than the average high school graduate, even after subtracting the cost of college. But it should not be *too* reassuring, because the economic payback to university graduates is not the only—or even the primary—aim of a university education.

To know whether a university education is worthwhile, we need to identify and defend the mission of a university education. Call this the mission question: what should universities aim to achieve for individuals and society? I answer the mission question for the sector of higher education I know best, selective colleges and universities; but there is reason to believe that these answers are also generally applicable to less selective colleges and universities, including many public universities and community colleges. I begin by asking: what is our ethical mission with regard to educating undergraduates?

In answering the question, I defend three fundamental aims of an undergraduate education in the twenty-first century:

- The first aim speaks to who is educated and calls for broader access to higher education based on talent and hard work, rather than income and wealth: in short, *opportunity*.
- The second aim speaks to the core intellectual aim of a university education, which I will argue calls for a greater integration of knowledge not only within the liberal arts and sciences, but also between the liberal arts and professional education: in short, *creative understanding*.
- The third aim, and an important sequel to the second, is enabling and encouraging university graduates to contribute to society on the basis of their creative understanding: in short, *contribution*.

Although the challenges of increasing opportunity, creative understanding, and contribution are not new, they take on renewed urgency in today's climate. Jobs are scarce. The United States is perceived to be declining in global competitiveness, and part of the problem is insufficient progress in education, starting with preschool and K–12 education.

Anyone who craves a simple or single pathway to educational and economic success will be disappointed. ("There is an easy solution to every human problem," H. L. Mencken quipped, "neat, plausible, and wrong.")[5] There are many external obstacles to educational and economic opportunity in the United States today—poverty, broken families, cutbacks in public support—that warrant everyone's attention. But taking to heart the ethical injunction "physician, heal thyself," I focus on what universities themselves can do to better realize their primary aims.

Starting with the first: what can universities do to help increase educational opportunity? Ironically, if Gross and Thiel are correct in assuming that a university education is generally a waste of time and money, then increasing access to a university education would be an even greater waste of time and money. But the best available evidence indicates that they are mistaken. According to a recent Brookings Institution study, college is "expensive, but a smart choice."[6] I would add: for those who have the choice—and everyone who has the potential to succeed should be afforded the choice. "Almost 90% of young college graduates were employed in 2010, compared with only 64% of their peers who did not attend college . . . [C]ollege graduates are making on average almost double the annual earnings of those with only a high school diploma. And this advantage is likely to stick with them over a lifetime of work."[7] Moreover, "the investment in college has a rate of return of a whopping 15.2% a year on the $102,000 investment for those who earn the average salary for college graduates."[8]

The most relevant (and indisputable) economic fact is that, even in the depths of the Great Recession, the unemployment rate of college graduates was less than half that of high school graduates and never exceeded 5.1 percent.[9] The more affordable universities make their education to qualified young people from low- and middle-income families, the more they contribute to both educational and economic opportunity.[10]

But this does not mean that the benefits of a college education accrue only—or even overwhelmingly—from increased economic opportunity. The second core intellectual aim of a university education highlights the benefits to college graduates of the lifelong satisfactions of creative understanding.

For low- and middle-income students, gainful employment itself is likely to be the most basic *economic* advantage of a college degree because the benefits of creative understanding are far harder to enjoy without basic economic security, and low- and middle-income students do not have a family nest egg of savings to draw upon in hard economic times. This observation does not require that the economic benefits of a university education be considered paramount among all the benefits of higher education. It does follow that—other things being equal—universities provide even greater value-added opportunity to low- and middle-income students. It is also true that opening the door to creative understanding can have even more profound effects on an individual's lifelong satisfaction, whether that door is framed by ivy or hung in less selective two-year, four-year, and community colleges. While selective universities cannot do everything—their core competency limits their ability to engage in compensatory education (one great advantage of community colleges and some less selective institutions)—the

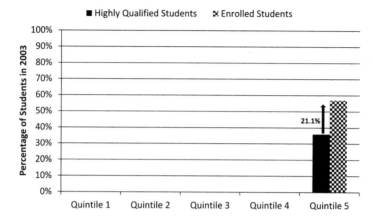

Fig. 1. The Big Squeeze.
The black bar shows the percentage of all highly qualified high school graduates who come from the wealthiest 20 percent of the population (36 percent). The checked bar shows the percentage of all students enrolled at highly selective colleges and universities who come from the 20 percent of the population with the highest incomes (57 percent), showing that among students with high academic qualifications, those from the top of the income distribution are overrepresented at highly selective institutions.
Source: Consortium on Financing Higher Education, 2003.

available data show that they can provide greater access to qualified students from low- and middle-income families than they have in the past.

My concern for increasing access began with a focus on recruiting qualified students from the lowest income groups.[11] Learning more led to the conclusion that increasing access for middle-income students should be a high priority.[12] I began by asking: what proportion of students on a set of selective university campuses (which included the University of Pennsylvania) come from the top 20 percent of American families as measured by income? The answer (as of 2003) was 57 percent.

Since all colleges and universities should admit only students who can succeed once admitted, selective colleges and universities also need to ask: what percentage of all students who are well qualified come from the wealthiest 20 percent? Thirty-six percent of all highly qualified seniors (with high grades and combined SATs over 1200) come from the top 20 percent, while 57 percent of selective-university students come from this group. The wealthiest 20 percent of American families are overrepresented on our campuses by a margin of 21 percent.

All other income groups are underrepresented. Students from the lowest 40 percent of the income distribution, whose families earn under about

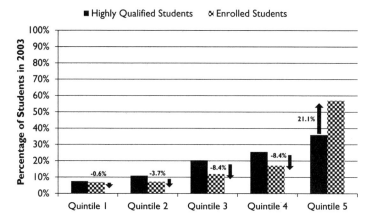

Fig. 2. The Big Squeeze, with more detail.
The bars show for each quintile of the income distribution what percentage of highly qualified high school graduates are in that quintile (black bars) and what percentage of students at highly selective colleges and universities are in that quintile (checkered bars). We see that highly qualified students from the four lower quintiles of the income distribution are underrepresented at elite institutions, whereas highly qualified students in the top quintile are overrepresented.
Source: Consortium on Financing Higher Education, 2003.

$41,000, are underrepresented by 4.3 percent. The middle 20 percent, who come from families earning $41,000 to $61,000, are underrepresented by 8.4 percent. Students from the second-highest income group, whose families earn between $62,000 and $94,000, are also underrepresented by 8.4 percent.

We need more than these numbers to make the case for increasing access. We also need narratives that highlight what is lost when a campus has few students from middle- and low-income families. The low- and middle-income students at the University of Pennsylvania whose peers are most underrepresented include:

· A young man from Illinois described by his advisor as the "ideal liberal arts student," with interests ranging from physics to international politics to literature to foreign languages. He is also a talented bass clarinetist. He has four siblings, including one with Down syndrome, and was raised by a single mother whose income is limited to Social Security and nominal child support. He required a cash advance from the University of Pennsylvania to buy his plane ticket to move to campus.

· A young woman from Connecticut who aspires to become an industrial-organizational psychologist, volunteers with an AIDS organization, and was an active participant in her school's Black Student League. Her mother recently lost the job she had held for twenty-five years and is fighting foreclosure on their home.

· A young man from South Dakota who plans to study psychology. His mother is a Head Start teacher on a Native American reservation. His advisor wrote that he had difficulty participating in high school activities because state budget cuts required parents to "contribute" to extracurricular programs and his mother had no income to spare for these pursuits.

· A young woman from Pennsylvania who wants to study neuroscience and behavioral psychology and has a growing interest in environmental studies and "green" issues. An active fund-raiser for community organizations, she has three siblings, including another in college. Her parents both work, one as a supermarket cashier and the other in a factory.

Increasing access to our universities for middle- and low-income students is both an especially worthy, and an increasingly daunting, challenge in the wake of the Great Recession. Before the recession, taking financial aid into account, middle- and low-income families were spending between 25 percent and 55 percent of their annual income to cover the expense of a public four-year college education.[13] That burden has skyrocketed over the past three years, especially for middle-income students, who are ineligible for Pell grants and who attend public universities whose public funding has been slashed.

A student from a typical middle-income family today will pay less to attend the University of Pennsylvania than many flagship public universities. Yet private universities also have experienced a big financial squeeze. Only by making financial aid one of their highest priorities and successfully raising many millions of dollars from generous donors can most private institutions afford to admit students on a need-blind basis and provide financial aid that meets full need. This may be the reason only about 1 percent of America's four thousand colleges and universities are committed to need-blind admissions *and* to meeting the full financial need of their undergraduate students. An even smaller group of universities is committed not only to meeting the full financial need of all students who are admitted on a need-blind basis, but also to providing financial aid *exclusively on the basis of need*. They thereby maximize the use of scarce aid dollars for students with demonstrated financial need.

In order to maximize its ability to increase opportunity through the Great Recession, the University of Pennsylvania lowered its costs to all students from families with demonstrated financial need. From 2004 to 2012 the average price of a University of Pennsylvania education for all students with demonstrated financial need *decreased* by $2,900 (in constant dollars). The University of Pennsylvania also instituted an all-grant/no-loan policy, substituting cash grants for loans for all undergraduates eligible for financial aid. This policy enables middle- and low-income students to graduate free of debt and opens up a world of career possibilities to graduates who would otherwise feel tremendous pressure to pick the highest paying rather than the most satisfying and worthy careers.[14]

Financial aid is not the only obstacle to increasing opportunity. Many middle- and low-income students perceive many selective private universities as not only unaffordable, but also unwelcoming. Outreach campaigns to underrepresented students, families, and secondary schools are essential to shift these misconceptions. In addition to visiting many schools that are not traditional "feeders" to the University of Pennsylvania, the university translated its admissions and financial aid materials into Spanish for non-English-speaking parents of Latino students. We have teamed up with the Knowledge is Power Program (KIPP) secondary schools and with the QuestBridge program, whose primary mission is to prepare low-income students—often minorities and the first in their families to attend college—for success at selective universities.

Although much more work remains, the University of Pennsylvania has significantly increased the proportion of first-generation, low- and middle-income, and underrepresented minority students on campus. One out of seven members of Penn's freshman class will be—like me—the first in their family to graduate from college. The percentage of underrepresented minorities at the University of Pennsylvania has increased from 15 percent to 22 percent over the past eight years. Minorities (including Asian Americans) account for almost half of the school's student body. After they arrive, many campus-wide initiatives enable these students to feel more at home and to succeed. Graduation rates for all groups are above 90 percent.

The positive impact of increasing opportunity extends beyond the low- and middle-income students who are admitted. Increased socioeconomic and racial diversity enriches the educational experience for everyone on a campus by promoting greater appreciation for life experiences and perspectives that differ from those that prevail among the most privileged.

Although I've mentioned the potential impact of increasing access and reducing financial barriers to well-qualified but underrepresented students in selective universities, it is important to note that the barriers—perceptual, financial, and psychological—to access are often significantly lower and the rewards similarly great for students at less selective schools. The logic of the argument applies *mutatis mutandis*.

This observation speaks to the second ethical aim of a university education: cultivating creative understanding. Students and their parents are understandably concerned about their immediate job prospects. Universities certainly should want to help them qualify for gainful employment; but we need to do much more for our students than prepare them for a job or career. The primary goal of universities is to educate students to understand their world creatively and constructively. Creative understanding is in turn a prerequisite to the third aim of an undergraduate education: graduating students who can act in a well-informed way to benefit society. These two aims apply across all sectors of higher education.

Most universities today embrace the idea of interdisciplinary learning in order to provide students with a more comprehensive understanding of the world beyond that which any single discipline can provide. Students are typically required to have in-depth knowledge in their major and to distribute their elective courses across the humanities, social sciences, and sciences (or in some cases, core courses) to broaden their understanding. Increasingly, students are being offered interdisciplinary majors that help them integrate knowledge across the traditional liberal arts and sciences disciplines ("liberal arts," for short). This integration among the liberal arts disciplines is a welcome development from the perspective of cultivating students' capacity to understand and respond creatively to complex social problems. Whether the issue is health care or human rights, unemployment or immigration, educational attainment or economic inequality, it cannot be comprehended—let alone effectively addressed—by the tools of only one academic discipline, no matter how masterly its methods or powerful its paradigms.

Consider, for example, the issue of climate change in a world that is both more interconnected and more populous than ever before. To be prepared to make a positive difference in this world, students must understand not only the science of sustainable design and development, but also the economic, political, and other issues in play. The key to solving every complex problem—climate change being one among many—will require connecting knowledge across multiple areas of expertise to both broaden and deepen creative understanding.

Nothing here suggests that the integration of knowledge should stop at the traditional boundaries of the liberal arts, especially since these boundaries have shifted—slowly but continually—over time. In my own field of political philosophy, for example, a scholarly approach centered on intellectual history ceded significant ground in the 1970s to critical analyses of contemporary public affairs, which was a paradigm common to many earlier generations of political philosophers. Were the liberal arts motivated solely by the pursuit of knowledge for its own sake, and not by any concern for worldly relevance, then it would be hard to make sense of such shifts. In the case of this important shift in political philosophy, scholars thought it valuable, in the face of ongoing injustice, to revive a tradition of ethical understanding and criticism of society. The ability of disciplines to change over time in response to such insight is critical to the educational importance of the liberal arts for students in every kind of academic institution.

A liberal arts education is the broadest kind of undergraduate education the modern world has known, and that breadth is an integral part of its power to generate creative understanding. But it is a mistake—judging by the ideal of intellectual creativity—to accept the conventional boundaries of a liberal arts education as fixed, rather than as a humanly alterable product of particular historical conditions. These conditions in the United States gave rise to a starker separation between the liberal arts and professional education than is intellectually ideal. To cultivate creative understanding about climate change, for example, chemical engineering—which is not a traditional liberal arts discipline nor even conventionally considered part of the liberal arts (engineering is typically classified as "professional or pre-professional education")—is just as important as economics or political science.

Today the broad area of professional ethics holds out enormous potential for intellectually enriching the liberal arts. This potential is well illustrated at the intersection of medical ethics and public policy. In my own scholarly career and more recently as chair of President Barack Obama's Presidential Commission for the Study of Bioethical Issues (also known as the Bioethics Commission), I have been involved in considering many challenging issues surrounding the ethics of health care and human-subjects research, almost none of which were part of a traditional liberal arts curriculum or education. How is health care most equitably distributed? What constitutes a conflict of interest for medical professionals? Why is it so ethically challenging to conduct human experiments, and how can they be justifiably conducted at all? These and a host of other intellectually challenging issues in bioethics will become even more salient as the science of medicine advances, the costs of health care potentially skyrocket, and the world grows more populous and interconnected.

It is not surprising, then, that one of the recommendations made by the Bioethics Commission in its 2011 report on the ethics of human-subjects research is that medical ethics be taught at the undergraduate level.[15] Any liberal arts curriculum would be strengthened by challenging students to understand not only what was specifically wrong in historic examples of unethical research, but also—and just as important—by enabling students to consider proactively how contemporary society can best protect individuals against unethical practices in the increasingly impactful field of human-subjects research. Educated people will be able to grapple with such difficult questions, which are essential to holding professionals publicly accountable, only if the subject is rigorously taught—and not just in professional schools or elite universities. Educators with a passion for the liberal arts can welcome such subjects into the curriculum and ensure that intellectually challenging and practically significant subjects, such as the ethics of the professions, not remain the primary—let alone the exclusive—province of professional education.

The problem with the strict separation between the liberal arts and subjects directly related to professional practice stems not from the fact that many liberal arts undergraduates plan to become professionals, but rather from the fact that *all* lives and societies will be profoundly shaped by the actions, attitudes, ethos, and ethics of the professions of law, medicine, nursing, business, engineering, and education, as well as the technological and trade disciplines less commonly found in the most selective institutions. Nonetheless, few undergraduates are taught to think deeply and systematically about the social roles and responsibilities of the professions and professionals. Just as teaching about politics helps to prepare students for thinking creatively about the role of politics in their lives and the life of their society and about how best to hold politicians accountable to serving the public, so too teaching about the ethics, history, politics, and sociology of the professions would help prepare students to think creatively about the role of the professions in society and how best to hold professionals publicly accountable.

A liberal arts degree is a prerequisite to professional education, and most liberal arts universities and their faculties stand firmly on the proposition that the liberal arts should inform the professions. Why then are liberal arts curricula not replete with courses that teach students to think carefully, critically, and creatively about the roles and responsibilities of professionals and the professions? Perhaps we are assuming that students will make these connections for themselves or that it will suffice if professional schools do so later. Neither assumption can be sustained.

First, we must not assume that students themselves will translate ethics as typically taught in a philosophy curriculum into the roles and responsibilities of the medical, business, and legal professions. The ethical considerations are too complex and profoundly affected by the institutional roles and responsibilities of professionals. Many lawyers, for example, are part of an adversarial system of justice; many doctors are part of a system in which they benefit financially from procedures that are not paid for directly by their patients; and many businesspeople operate in what is commonly called a free market, where external interferences are (rightly or wrongly) presumed prima facie to be suspect. These and many other contextual considerations profoundly complicate the practical ethics of law, medicine, and business.

Second, while the mission of professional schools is to prepare liberal arts graduates to become responsible members of their professions, it does not follow that professional schools should be the exclusive province of teaching and research directly concerned with the professions. Both individuals and societies are profoundly affected by the complex interconnections between medicine, business, and law on the one hand, and ethics, economics, and politics on the other.

My primary point is this: although the separation of the liberal arts from the subject of professional roles and responsibilities may be taken for granted because it is so conventional, it really should strike us as strange, on both intellectual and educational grounds, that so few courses in the undergraduate curriculum explicitly relate the liberal arts to professional life. This is a puzzle worthy of both intellectual and practical solution.

In *The Marketplace of Ideas*, Louis Menand addresses this puzzle and offers the most powerful historical explanation of how and why this separation occurred in American higher education. The separation was driven by three factors: the historical evolution of American higher education, a powerful advocate in late nineteenth-century higher education, and a mutually convenient (rather than educationally compelling) division of labor between liberal arts and professional educators.[16]

The historical account takes us back to a time in the United States when a liberal arts education was the exclusive domain of the American elite, who looked down upon all practically oriented education. Practically oriented professional education grew up separately alongside liberal arts education in the United States. Not until the late nineteenth century did a liberal arts degree become the gateway to the professions. In 1868, for example:

> Only 19 of the 411 medical students at the University of Michigan, and none of the 387 law students there, had prior degrees of any kind. There were no

admissions requirements at Harvard Law School, beyond evidence of "good character" and the ability to pay the hundred dollars tuition, which went into the pockets of the law professors. There were no grades or exams.[17]

In 1869, when Charles Eliot began his forty years as Harvard's president, he brought "one original and revolutionary idea with him . . . to make the bachelor's degree a prerequisite for admission to professional school." Eliot's idea of making a liberal arts education the exclusive gateway to the professions was a "key element in the transformation of American higher education in the decades after the Civil War."[18] It had two long-term effects. The first was to "put universities in the exclusive business of credentialing professionals."[19] The second was to enable liberal arts colleges to preserve their "anti-utilitarian ethos in an increasingly secular and utilitarian age."[20] "The practical spirit and the literary or scholastic spirit are both good, but they are incompatible," Eliot argued; "if commingled, they are both spoiled."[21]

This stark separation of the practical and theoretical was not an inevitable outgrowth of earlier educational efforts, nor has it ever been universally accepted. In fact, it flew in the face of at least one early American effort to integrate the liberal arts and professional education. In his educational blueprint entitled "Proposals Relating to the Education of Youth in Pensilvania," which later led to the founding of the University of Pennsylvania, Benjamin Franklin called for students to be taught "every Thing that is useful, and every Thing that is ornamental." Being a principled pragmatist, Franklin immediately addressed the obvious rejoinder that no educational institution can teach everything. And so, he continued, "Art is long, and their Time is short. It is therefore propos'd that they learn those Things that are likely to be most useful and most ornamental."[22]

Franklin's admirable efforts at integration notwithstanding, the dominant historical development of liberal arts and professional education in the United States followed Eliot's separatist philosophy: "utility . . . everywhere in the professional schools but nowhere in the colleges."[23] Liberal arts education, Eliot insisted, must be "the enthusiastic study of subjects for the love of them without any ulterior objects, the love of learning and research for their own sake."[24]

As the separation between liberal arts and professional education unfolded over time, the liberal arts—not surprisingly—turned out to be less pure in practice than Eliot's separatist dictum prescribed. For example, professional schools declared some undergraduate courses—such as organic chemistry—as prerequisites, which immediately imparted to these courses an intended practical purpose. But the general aversion to practical subjects, and the suspicion of practical motivations for learning, already had been deeply implanted in liberal arts culture, with the consequence of making every "impure" part of the liberal arts curriculum seem polluted for being "preprofessional." Often such prerequisite courses are considered less admirable because students are assumed to be taking them only for instrumental reasons.

In addition, the unfolding of the liberal arts curriculum charged undergraduates with choosing a major out of intellectual passion, not for a practical or professional purpose, lest the liberal arts spirit of learning for its own sake be spoiled by practical or professional purposes. Like prerequisite courses, those majors that became natural feeders to professional schools—economics to business school, political science to law, biology to medical school—also were expected to defend their reputations against becoming preprofessional. Premedical students majoring in biology, prelaw students in political science, and prebusiness students in economics were suspected of having less worthy motivations for their studies than classics, math, or physics majors.

Despite these concerns regarding the separation between liberal arts and professional education, we still can recognize that something educationally significant is lost if students choose their majors for purely professional reasons, rather than because they want to be both well educated *and* well prepared for a likely future career. The introduction of distribution requirements for all majors is one way of responding to this potential problem.

An equally powerful response is for liberal arts educators—and this is a lesson to be learned from those who teach in less selective institutions—to acknowledge that few people are so economically privileged that they can afford to be motivated solely by the love of learning for its own sake. As undergraduates, most students (whether in selective universities, community colleges, or anywhere in between) need to prepare for gainful and socially productive employment, and there should not be a scintilla of shame in choosing a major because it helps to prepare you for a profession or career if you also are genuinely interested in broadly pursuing what the subject matter has to offer. Save for the few saints among us, most people have mixed motivations in pursuing the significant goals in their lives.

Make no mistake: we should strive to ensure that the liberal arts not succumb to encouraging an exclusively professional motivation for undergraduate education. Part of the glory of an American liberal arts education is the way it enables undergraduates to keep their intellectual sights and their career options open while cultivating intellectual curiosity and creativity that will enhance any of the career paths they later choose to follow. Courses and majors are typically designed so that they are compatible with many career paths and spark students' intellectual creativity rather than narrow their imaginations. These are among the most eminently defensible aims of a liberal arts education: to broaden rather than narrow the sights of undergraduates, and to strengthen rather than stifle their creative potential. But both of these aims admit of intellectually creative, preprofessional education at every point along the institutional spectrum. Both aims, for example, would argue in favor of including courses in the undergraduate curriculum on the social role and responsibility of the professions.

For some of the same reasons that we should staunchly defend the liberal arts against becoming narrowly preprofessional, we also should build on Franklin's integrated vision and oppose a rigid separation (à la Eliot) of the "scholastic" and the "practical" spirit. Separating the two spirits is a means of stifling rather than stoking creative understanding, since so much that provokes our creative understanding straddles the worlds of theory and practice, and the professions are a large part of both worlds. The insights that the liberal arts can offer to the professions are also great—as is the creative challenge of integrating these insights into professional practice.

The professed ideal of keeping the liberal arts separate from preprofessional education also smacks of self-deception. As Menand points out, liberal arts majors are actually preprofessional for one small segment of the undergraduate population—future professors—although only a tiny minority of undergraduates ever will enter the professoriate.

Additionally, the separation between the liberal arts and professional education—along with its departmental divisions—has endured because the separation has become institutionally useful for some significant purposes. It enables universities to organize departments (roughly) around academic disciplines, which is a useful way to educate graduate students and recruit faculty members. It helps faculty members in a broad discipline or subject matter to organize courses that introduce students to the range of knowledge and methods needed to develop in-depth understanding.

This rationale does not in itself justify the continued maintenance of a rigid and impermeable wall between the liberal arts and the professions. The mistake is multiplied because the institutional separation of the liberal arts and professional education has created something akin to "an allergy to the term 'vocational.'"[25] And anything that concerns any profession other than academia itself is considered "vocational." The separation also has engendered among many defenders of the liberal arts a quasi-instinctual opposition to any undergraduate "curriculum designed with real-world goals in mind."[26] All of applied ethics, therefore—not just professional ethics—

may be tainted for being too practical (that is, not sufficiently theoretical) in its aims.

I propose that we proudly defend a liberal arts education as broadly pre-professional and optimally instrumental in the pursuit of real-world goals. At its best, a liberal arts education prepares undergraduates for success in whatever profession they choose to pursue, and it does so by means of teaching them to think creatively and critically about themselves, their society (including the roles and responsibilities of the professions in their society), and the world.

One good reason to emphasize the importance of the love of learning for its own sake is that these real-world goals cannot always be best achieved directly. When we pursue knowledge for its own sake, we stretch our imaginations and our time horizons. We do not expect what we learn will quickly "pay off."

The love of higher learning for its own sake, however, cannot and should not be the exclusive aim of a liberal arts education. It cannot be the exclusive aim because it is impossible to distinguish between the love of learning for its own sake and for the sake of making a positive difference in the world. It should not be the exclusive aim because it is not always more effective in producing creative thinking to teach students by indirection. The practical point of a liberal arts education—understanding how best to tackle complex and important (empirical and ethical) problems—can effectively pique creative thinking, along with the love of learning.

By integrating the liberal arts with a deeper and broader understanding of the professions, universities would better prepare students for facing up to the challenges of their private, professional, and civic lives. Conversely, universities are letting their students and society down when they leave the complex connections between the liberal arts and professions to be made later in life—or not at all.

The time has come to break down the rigid divide between the liberal arts and the professions. Bridging this divide would be as revolutionary today as creating the divide was in Eliot's time, and similarly important.

To the extent that twenty-first-century universities recognize this divide as an institutional convenience (or inconvenience) rather than as an intellectual asset, we can build more productive intellectual bridges between the liberal arts and professional education. We can show how insights gained from history, philosophy, literature, politics, economics, sociology, and science enrich understandings of law, business, medicine, nursing, engineering, architecture, and education—and how professional understandings can in turn enrich insights into liberal arts disciplines. We can demonstrate that understanding the roles and responsibilities of professionals in society is an important part of the higher education of democratic citizens.

This leads naturally to the third aim of a university education: maximizing the social contribution of universities based on their core competencies. One of their core competencies is the ability of a liberal arts education to cultivate creative understanding, which in turn enables educated individuals to make key contributions to society.

In the twenty-first century, the unprecedented social power of knowledge-driven professions makes cultivating the creative understanding of professionals key to universities' contributing to society based on their core intellectual competencies. Universities are engines of both individual empowerment and social progress. The very same creative understanding that empowers individuals to lead productive lives as citizens and professionals also generates social progress.

To avoid any complacency about the university's mission of undergraduate education that would stifle social progress, I have focused on an increasingly important but often neglected way in which the liberal arts can maximize their social contribution: by broadening their reach to better comprehend the roles and responsibilities of the professions for talented students from all walks of life. Because the professions profoundly affect the lives of all citizens, teaching students about their social roles and responsibilities should not begin at the professional-school level—or even be restricted to the most selective colleges and universities. For the many undergraduates who plan to become professionals, it is equally important to introduce them early to this subject in a learning context, where fellow professionals are not the only ones taking part in the educational dialogue.

There are many other ways in which all colleges and universities contribute to society by cultivating creative understanding. They also can model ethical responsibility and social service in their institutional practices and initiatives. Their capital investments in educational facilities contribute to the economic progress of their local communities. Colleges and universities at every level can be institutional models of environmental sustainability in the way they build and maintain their campuses.

The core social contribution of universities in the realm of undergraduate liberal arts education depends on the progress made both in increasing opportunity for students and in cultivating their creative understandings. Similarly, the analogous core social contributions of universities in the realms of faculty research and clinical service depend on better integrating insights across the liberal arts and the professions.

At the University of Pennsylvania, in the spirit of Franklin, our founder, there is far-ranging receptivity by faculty, students, and alumni alike to bridging intellectual and institutional divides that for several centuries have separated the liberal arts and professional education. It is increasingly evident how much creative understanding there is to be gained, and how little of intellectual importance there is to be lost, by embracing the integration of knowledge.

To return to the fundamental question: what makes an undergraduate education worthwhile? An education that cultivates creative understanding enables diverse, talented, hardworking graduates to pursue productive careers, enjoy the pleasures of lifelong learning, and reap the satisfactions of creatively contributing to society. The corresponding institutional mission of colleges and universities at all levels is to increase opportunity, to cultivate creative understanding, and—by these and other important means such as innovative research and clinical service—to contribute to society. At their best, universities recruit hardworking, talented, and diverse student bodies and help them develop the understandings—including the roles and responsibilities of the professions in society—that are needed to address complex social challenges in the twenty-first century. To the extent that universities do this and do it well, we can confidently say to our students and our society that a university education is a wise investment indeed.

Notes

1. http://www.pimco.com/EN/Insights/Pages/School-Daze-School-Daze-Good-Old-Golden-Rule-Days.aspx (accessed September 20, 2011). Questioning the value of a college degree is nothing new. In *Pudd'nhead Wilson*, Mark Twain quipped that "cauliflower is nothing but cabbage with a college education." Mark Twain, *The Tragedy of Pudd'nhead Wilson* (Hartford, CT: American, 1894), 67.
2. See press release at http://www.thielfellowship.org/news/tf-press-releases/ (accessed January 3, 2012).
3. See, e.g., Greg Ip, "The Declining Value of Your College Degree," *Wall Street Journal*, July 17, 2008, http://online.wsj.com/article/SB121623686919059307.html (accessed September 21, 2011); Louis Menand, "Live and Learn: Why We Have College," *New Yorker*, June 6, 2011, http://www.newyorker.com/arts/critics/atlarge/2011/06/06/110606crat_atlarge_menand (accessed September 21, 2011); Daniel Indiviglio, "The Importance of College: A Self-Fulfilling Prophecy," *Atlantic*, June 27, 2011, http://www.theatlantic.com/business/archive/2011/06/the-importance-of-college-a-self-fulfilling-prophecy/241092/ (accessed September 21, 2011); and Michael Greenstone and Adam Looney, "College: Expensive, but a Smart Choice," *Los Angeles Times*, August 15, 2011, http://articles.latimes.com/2011/aug/15/opinion/la-oe-looney-greenstone-is-college-wo20110815 (accessed September 21, 2011).

4. See, e.g., Sandy Baum, Jennifer Ma, and Kathleen Payea, *Education Pays 2010: The Benefits of Higher Education for Individuals and Society* ([New York]: College Board Advocacy & Policy Center, 2010); Anthony P. Carnevale, Jeff Strohl, and Michelle Melton, *What's It Worth: The Economic Value of College Majors* ([Washington, DC: Georgetown University Center for Education and the Workforce, 2011); Greenstone and Looney, "College: Expensive, but a Smart Choice"; and Kevin Carey, "Bad Job Market: Why the Media Is Always Wrong about the Value of a College Degree," *New Republic* blog, http://www.tnr.com/article/economy/89675/bad-job-market-media-wrong-college-degree?id=c3tDkrWcVzH3jltcgTA2oTDTydf5y5q6/J8/xDMU1/53nKY+kSwzHmksnbcDeVk/ (accessed September 20, 2011).

5. H. L. Mencken, *A Mencken Chrestomathy* (New York: A. A. Knopf, 1949), 443.

6. Greenstone and Looney, "College: Expensive, but a Smart Choice."

7. Ibid.

8. Ibid.

9. Labor Force Statistics from the Current Population Survey, U.S. Department of Labor, Bureau of Labor Statistics.

10. We also know that the economic returns of some majors, such as English and education, are far smaller than those of others, such as economics and engineering. But even with these qualifications, individuals still stand to gain—both economically and in other ways—from graduating college; see, e.g., Carnevale, Strohl, and Melton, *What's It Worth*.

11. See, e.g., Michael S. McPherson and Morton Owen Schapiro, "Does Student Aid Affect College Enrollment? New Evidence on a Persistent Controversy," *American Economic Review* 81, no. 1 (1991), 309–18; Michael S. McPherson and Morton Owen Schapiro, "The Student Finance System for Undergraduate Education: How Well Does It Work?" *Change* 23, no. 3 (1991), 16–22; Michael S. McPherson and Morton Owen Schapiro, "Financing Undergraduate Education: Designing National Policies," National Center for Postsecondary Improvement, 1997; and Michael S. McPherson and Morton Owen Schapiro, eds., *College Access: Opportunity or Privilege?* (New York: College Board, 2006).

12. According to a 2008 report published by the National Center for Public Policy and Higher Education (and funded by the Bill and Melinda Gates and Lumina Foundations), 91 percent of high school students from families making over $100,000 a year enroll in college. The enrollment rate for students from middle-class families—those earning between $50,000 and $100,000 a year—is 78 percent. And for students from families in the lowest income bracket, $20,000 and below, the rate is 52 percent. National Center for Public Policy and Higher Education, "Measuring Up 2008: National and State Report Cards on Higher Education."

13. National Center for Public Policy and Higher Education, "Measuring Up 2008: The National Report Card on Higher Education." http://measuringup2008.highereducation.org/ (accessed September 21, 2011).

14. Penn was able to implement and sustain a need-blind, need-based, no-loan financial aid program despite having an endowment that ranks fifty-seventh in size per capita in recent data provided by the National Association of College and University Business Officers (NACUBO). One possible lesson is that other universities—with proportionally more resources—can also increase aid for low- and middle-income students if they make need-based financial aid one of their highest institutional priorities.

15. Presidential Commission for the Study of Bioethical Issues, "Moral Science: Pro-

tecting Participants in Human Subjects Research," http://www.bioethics.gov/cms/node/558 (accessed January 9, 2012). The Bioethics Commission is developing a study guide to its earlier report (entitled *Ethically Impossible*) that details grotesque human-rights abuses by American researchers who conducted experiments sponsored by the United States government in Guatemala from 1946 to 1948.

16. Louis Menand, *The Marketplace of Ideas: Reform and Resistance in the American University* (New York: Norton, 2010).

17. "To get an MD at Harvard, students were obliged to take a ninety-minute oral examination, during which nine students rotated among nine professors, . . . spending ten minutes with each. . . . Any student who passed five of the nine fields became a doctor." Ibid., 46.

18. Ibid., 45.

19. Ibid., 47.

20. Ibid., 49.

21. Charles Eliot, "The New Education, I," *Atlantic Monthly*, February 1869, 215.

22. Benjamin Franklin, "Proposals Relating to the Education of Youth in Pensilvania, Philadelphia, 1749," http://www.archives.upenn.edu/primdocs/1749proposals.html (accessed September 21, 2011).

23. Menand, *The Marketplace of Ideas*, 49.

24. Eliot, "The New Education, I," 214. See also Hugh Hawkins, *Between Harvard and America: The Educational Leadership of Charles W. Eliot* (New York: Oxford University Press, 1972).

25. Ibid, 53.

26. Ibid., 50.

THREE

Defending the Humanities in a Liberal Society

CHRISTOPHER BERTRAM

Introduction

Scholars of the arts and humanities have come to think of themselves as being increasingly under threat both in the United States and in my country, the United Kingdom.[1] The reasons for this are various. One is a perception that the wider society conceives of the humanities as somehow useless or frivolous, an unnecessary luxury at a time of economic retrenchment and relative decline. According to this view, social resources should be diverted instead into science, technology, engineering, and mathematics (STEM), since the future wealth and prosperity of nations depends on societies having enough people who are well educated and trained in those disciplines and who can contribute directly to economic growth. Choices by individuals, at least in the United States, partly reflect this perception, as the relative share of student enrollment in humanities is flat, and many students now pick majors with a clear vocational payoff instead.[2]

To these economic and social pressures on the humanities we can add a further source of anxiety both inside and outside the academy. Confidence in the humanities as the repositories of supposedly superior Western cultural values has largely disappeared. Except in a few culturally conservative circles, there is much less attachment than there once was to the idea of the objective superiority and unity of Western civilization, higher culture, and objective aesthetic values. Much of this loss of confidence has occurred for very good reasons and is based on more than a century of reaction to the wars and genocides of the past, and to the end of European colonial empires. Within the academy, this loss of cultural confidence has found expression in a loss of prestige for the canon of great books, a flirtation with (and occasional embrace of) various relativisms and subjectivisms, and a somewhat democratic and egalitarian refocusing of interest toward the experience and culture of ordinary people and to the art, history, and experience of non-Western societies. The combination of this loss of confidence in traditional values with the rise of a utilitarian concern with growth and prosperity has, unsurprisingly, raised questions about whether the humanities should retain their place in the academy and its curriculum.

At the same time, this crisis of the humanities has a certain paradoxical aspect because it comes when the areas of human experience that these subjects take as objects of study have become more central to most people's lives than they were in the past. Until recently most individuals, even in the Western world, spent the majority of their time preoccupied with the grim business of working in order to live and raise families. People lived shorter lives, and access to cultural goods was more limited than it is today. Though we may have reached a pause in the extension of leisure time, we still live in an era when, via media such as television, the Internet, and sound recordings, people have greatly increased the quantity and breadth of the drama and music they consume compared to their ancestors. The English critic Raymond Williams illustrates this strikingly: "It seems probable that in societies like Britain and the United States more drama is watched in a week or weekend, by the majority of viewers, than would have been watched in a year or in some cases a lifetime in any previous historical period . . . to put it categorically, most people spend more time watching various kinds of drama than in preparing or eating food."[3]

The content of this contemporary imaginative world is often also the result of the importation and combination of the products of many different cultures, countries, and languages. This makes a richness of cultural experience available to individuals, at least potentially, that only elites could enjoy in the premodern age. This centrality of the arts is, of course, not a feature of our consumption time alone. It also impinges on the production of what we watch and listen to and of the things we use in our everyday lives. The creative expression and humanistic insight of artists, photographers, writers, musicians, and designers is channeled into the making of television programs, films, and advertising, and into the design of the most mundane household objects. The new world we live in is not, then, just the creation of scientists and engineers, but results from the collaboration of people who possess technical and scientific knowledge with others who have a flair for artistic expression. Given this more prominent place of the arts in the imaginative life of the population and their indispensable role in the appearance and "feel" of the contemporary world, the sense of embattlement on the part of humanities scholars seems discordant.

In what follows, I explore some lines of defense and justification for the humanities. The first of these, familiar to anyone who has been listening to politicians in the United States or the United Kingdom over the past few decades, focuses on economic growth and development. According to this argument, the basic justification for education and research quite generally (and therefore for higher education as well) is to assist in the project of national material enrichment. Education aims to provide the workers the economy needs, and the purpose of research is to promote innovation and discovery so that "we" stay one step ahead of the competition. According to this outlook, if the arts and humanities are to retain their place, they will have to show that they contribute to economic growth. I conclude that whilst arguments directed to the well-being of citizens are perfectly in order, the specific growth-based form these have taken is far too narrow and gets in the way of the critical reflection to which the humanities can contribute.

The second line of defense agrees with my conclusion regarding growth: that this economic focus is mistaken and impoverished. After all, we are not just entrepreneurs and workers, but also citizens of democratic societies. If the humanities can be shown to have some essential role in the constitution of the citizens of such societies, perhaps by instilling in them democratic virtues or habits of mind, then we will have compelling reason to continue to support the study and teaching of them within the academy. Here I pay particular attention to the important arguments advanced by the University of Chicago philosopher Martha Nussbaum in a recent book.[4] However, whilst allowing that the humanities have a contribution to make to the democratic conversation of a people, I find Nussbaum's arguments unconvincing in some respects, largely because they claim too much.

A third set of arguments that relate to both the economic and political justifications, but is not reducible to either of them, concerns the way in which the humanities can keep alive a genuine diversity of views on ways to live and conceptions of the good in the face of strong societal pressures to uniformity. Though it would be wrong to put social resources in the service of any particular conception of the good, the preservation of choice in conceptions of the good is something in which citizens, as a whole, have an interest.

In the final section of this essay I advance a fourth set of arguments, the general thrust of which is an attempt to situate the humanities within the more general enterprise of advancing knowledge, both alongside the natural sciences and, in important ways, as complementary to them. This view of the humanities as part of the broad scientific enterprise has an instrumental component (as the example of medical humanities brings out) but also takes part in a general human interest in knowledge about our world as such. This defense does not necessarily lead to the conclusion that the provision of the humanities in the academy should continue in the same form that it traditionally has.

In what follows, I say very little about what the humanities are, presuming a rough consensus on the subjects we are talking about, even in the absence of a definition. If pressed, however, I would say something about their methodological unity. The humanities are that branch of inquiry that depends on interpretation and understanding in order to make sense of the world that human beings have made, of their culture, history, behavior, and artifacts. As such, it is not clear the humanities form a neatly compartmentalized domain, nor that they are reliably coextensive with the subjects that might be put in a university division of humanities for administrative purposes. There will be some parts of the social sciences that are humanistic in outlook or where both humanistic and more "scientific" approaches coexist, and there will be areas whose status is vague. Philosophy, for example, is not part of the humanities where it shades into mathematics but more clearly is in domains such as aesthetics and, perhaps, politics.

All of the above presupposes that we have some idea of the kinds of argument that would count as relevant to the defense and vindication of the humanities. I take as my starting point here the idea of liberal justification, as outlined over the past four decades by philosophers such as John Rawls and Ronald Dworkin. The precise specification of that ideal is a matter of philosophical controversy, and some philosophers and political theorists reject it altogether.[5] However, for the sake of argument, I shall take some version of that approach as specifying the kinds of justifications that are suitable for citizens to advance to one another concerning the deployment of public power and the nature of the basic institutions that they share. As I outline in the next section, there are both principled and pragmatic reasons to adopt this constraint on justification.

Liberal Justification

The liberal principle of legitimacy says that the policies of government and the institutions of society face a justificatory burden.[6] They have to be capable of being justified to all of those over whom state power is exercised. On this view of state power, the public power, the res publica, belongs to all of its citizens. As such, it may not be used to limit their freedom, except for reasons they accept, or, more plausibly, rationally ought to accept.[7] This creates a well-known difficulty in a pluralistic society, because there is a lack of consensus among citizens on many matters of basic value. Citizens differ profoundly in their tastes and preferences, in their religious and political affiliations, in many of the aesthetic and moral ideals they embrace, and, no doubt, on other relevant dimensions. Given this plurality of values and commitments, the justification of state power and action becomes problematic, since policy makers cannot, whilst respecting their fellow citizens as their democratic equals, advance arguments that depend on premises they know many people in their society not only do not accept, but have no good reason to accept. Legislation and policy making cannot, therefore, proceed on the basis that some religious standpoint, such as Roman Catholicism, is true, and legislators and judges cannot advance arguments based on Catholic doctrine or teaching as such, since many citizens do not accept and cannot be shown to have reason to accept such arguments.

The constraints of liberal justification may seem to leave the state paralyzed and simply unable to act within whole areas of human life, but arguably this appearance is misleading. The state *can* continue to act, but it must justify its actions in terms that appeal to the shared reason of citizens, to their public reason. This leaves available a series of justificatory possibilities, some aimed at the individual well-being or freedom of citizens and others at the continued existence and flourishing of the political collective of which they form a part and of its constitutive relationships. In relation to individual persons, the state may legitimately act so as to promote and expand the broadly conceived well-being, opportunities, and freedoms of its citizens on the grounds that whatever their particular view of where their good lies, their interests will be advanced, or at least not harmed, by the state. Under the more collective aspect, there are two main possibilities. First, the state can act so as to promote and defend the just associative relationships that citizens have with one another as free and equal beings. It can preserve the very framework within which they advance arguments toward one another and take collective decisions. It can act so as to ensure that some citizens are not subjected to oppressive domination by others. (Both the maximization of freedoms and opportunities and their fair distribution are therefore, in principle, within the domain of legitimate state action.) Second, and perhaps more controversial, the state can take account of psychological and sociological facts that bear on the unity and preservation of the political order. This might, in principle, justify a program of patriotic education, ceremonies of national unity and belonging, and even, in an extreme case, an established church.[8] This is not on the unacceptable grounds that the values thereby celebrated are the true ones, but rather because they turn out to be—as a matter of sociological fact—functionally necessary to preserve a just social and political order.

When it comes to higher education, this liberal justificatory framework might seem to bear somewhat differently on countries such as the United States, with its diverse mix of provision, much of which is privately funded, from states such as the United Kingdom, where, at least historically, most of the support higher education has received has come through general taxation. Universities in continental Europe are almost entirely dependent on taxpayer support. No doubt there are important differences among these systems, but perhaps fewer relevant ones than appear at first. The biggest is that insofar as the pattern and extent of provision of higher education is a consequence of people making private decisions with resources they are justly entitled to, the liberal principle of legitimacy is not breached. If a person in a liberal society chooses to donate her justly earned income to the foundation and support of institutes of Islamic studies on the grounds that she believes Islam to be the one true religion, then that is a private matter of no legitimate concern to others. If the state were to use common resources to do the same thing, that would be an injustice against followers of other religions.

However, there is a broader set of considerations in play. The first of these concerns is the capacity of private donors to seriously affect the provision of higher education. A highly unequal society, in which very wealthy donors are able to pursue philanthropic projects to the extent to which they do in the United States today, may itself be incompatible with the liberal order because of the way in which the economic inequality of citizens can undermine their political equality. In addition, the state is often implicated in such private donations via the tax concessions it makes with respect to charitable donations and its policy decisions regarding what counts as a charitable purpose. Such policies must pass the test of liberal justification. Second, the higher-education sector is an important part of what Rawls calls the "basic structure of society," which has huge effects on how citizens' lives turn out, both individually and compared to one another. As such, the state in all liberal societies has an interest in seeing to it that the aggregate effects of the operations of the sector are consonant with the demands of justice, whatever the degree to which the state is involved directly in educational provision. In this respect, the legitimate state interest in the regulation of higher education can be seen as being similar to its interest in the regulation of other industries and activities for the public benefit. Such examples include food hygiene regulations, safety standards, and regulation of the economy and tax system to ensure that individual choices do not unjustifiably erode equal opportunity or worsen the prospects of the least advantaged.

So what then, within this framework, of the arts and humanities? The liberal justificatory approach seems to rule out defenses of the arts and humanities within higher education or, at least, of state support and provision for them, that proceed from aesthetic, moral, or religious premises that many citizens cannot endorse, such as the objective superiority of the Western canon. Many commentators on recent developments have noticed this and bemoaned it. For example, in a series of articles in the *London Review of Books*, the British critic Stefan Collini portrays the shift from objective cultural values, as a justification for higher-education policy, to economic and political ones as being the ephemeral stuff of fashion:

> Very broadly speaking, the extension of democratic and egalitarian social attitudes has been accompanied by the growth of a kind of consumerist relativism. The claim that one activity is inherently of greater value or importance than another comes to be pilloried as "elitism." Arguments are downgraded to "opinions": all opinions are equally valuable (or valueless), so the only agreed-upon criterion is what people say they think they want, and the only value with any indefeasible standing is "value for money."[9]

But this seems wrong. The shift Collini is complaining about is best understood not as a mere change in fashion that might just as easily change back, but as part of a broadly justified change in the understanding of the reasons for study of the liberal arts that are applicable to public policy in a liberal and democratic society. Collini construes this change too narrowly, since economic benefit is not the only kind of value that can pass the test of liberal justification. However, he is wrong to reject the worries concerning elitism. Insofar as the arts and humanities rely upon things such as education policy, legislation, or the support of the taxpayer, and thereby also on the power of the state to conscript, coerce, and tax our fellow citizens, there are serious limits to the values that can be called upon to justify this. That a policy will, perhaps over the long term and by indirect means, provide people with more resources with which to pursue the aims they have chosen for themselves is the kind of justification we can imagine them accepting. Similarly, that the arts and humanities are in some way implicated in the formation of competent citizens or that they bolster sensitivity to matters of social justice is good liberal grounds for support. Objective aesthetic values are not: if fans of country music, for example, have a hard time understanding and accepting that they should pay taxes to support the study of Latin poetry or the works of Webern, it is not difficult to sympathize with them.

The approach adopted in this essay is, then, one of epistemic self-denial of the exclusion of certain reasons for action and policy. As such, it will strike some readers as irrational. Surely, they will say, policy should be based on all the best reasons applicable to an issue, rather than on an arbitrary subset of such reasons. Such complaints may have their basis in consequentialist theories that grant no distinctive importance to ideals of society as associations of free and equal citizens, who owe one another reasons in justification of coercion. Alternatively, they may come from perfectionist views, more inclined to defend the arts and humanities, for example, in terms that accord with their own self-image and the personal values of their scholars and practitioners. This is not the right place for a full adjudication of the merits and demerits of such competing approaches. I am inclined to defend the liberal justificatory approach on grounds of moral principle, on the basis that it is wrong and unjust to employ the coercive force of the state, in terms that could not be justified to those subject to it. However, for those unconvinced of the principled reasons behind such a stance, or perhaps skeptical of the notion that we can sort out all the difficulties involved with the idea of justification to a person, I would urge a more pragmatic case. In a democracy, we need to convince politicians and the electorate they represent, of the need to support higher education generally, the scientific enterprise broadly considered, and, within that, the arts and humanities. We stand more of a chance with that task if we can couch our arguments in terms they have good reason to find acceptable and comprehensible and can avow openly. From the perspective of this chapter, therefore, principle and pragmatism converge.

Justifying the Humanities on Economic Grounds

As should be clear from the previous section, one of the kinds of justification that looks at least prima facie justifiable in a liberal society is one focused on expanding the well-being, opportunities, and freedoms of citizens, improvements that might very plausibly occur through an increase in the wealth and income both of individuals and of the society as a whole. Such justifications have featured in prominent arguments around education policy, generally in both the United States and the United Kingdom. In the United Kingdom they have been central to recent policy discourse on higher education. As a result, in trying to mount a case for the arts and humanities, academics and their representative bodies have echoed these concerns, making the case that, far from being a luxury, these subjects can make a contribution to economic growth alongside the natural and applied sciences. Though these justifications are, in principle, acceptable in form, they suffer in practice from two related defects. First, they take it as settled that the goal of national policy should be economic growth in the narrow sense of the expansion of gross domestic product, and that this will bring jobs and prosperity to the population. Second, because they take that question as settled, they neglect other policy options that might do a better job of improving collective well-being. To make the first of these points is to say that the goals of public policy, including in the economic sphere, ought to be a matter for public argument and debate, and that, therefore, securing the conditions under which such argument and justification are possible has a logical priority over any particular policy objective. Accordingly, making participation in such argument possible ought to be one of the central concerns of the educational system generally, and of higher education in particular. If the arts and humanities can be shown to play an important role in this, then some of the business of justifying them will have been done. (I address the potential contribution of the arts and humanities to this in the next section.) To make the second point is to draw attention to policies, other than growth promotion, that may also contribute to the well-being and freedom of citizens and that the growth-promotion agenda tends to hide from us.

Though the United States, like other countries, has a rich tradition of thinking about the value and purpose of education, this tradition is not much in evidence in the public pronouncements of politicians. As an example, take a speech on education by President Barack Obama on March 10, 2009. There the focus is clear: education is the foundation of national prosperity, and America is falling behind other nations. Education should aim not just to provide all with valuable skills, but also to assist in an economic battle among nations. As President Obama puts it, "It is time to prepare every child, everywhere in America, to out-compete any worker, anywhere in the world."[10] In the United Kingdom, the so-called Browne Report, "Securing a Sustainable Future for Higher Education," is the underpinning of current higher-education policy. Commissioned by the Labour government before the 2010 general election, its terms of reference reflect a bipartisan consensus about the aims and purposes of universities. Although the report makes token reference to the fact that higher-education institutions "create the knowledge, skills and values that underpin a civilised society," the entire thrust of the more elaborate justifications it offers concern the competitive benefits to the United Kingdom of having a highly educated workforce and the personal benefits for individuals, construed in terms of career advancement and income, of having a university degree.[11] Browne, in this respect, represents the culmination of a trend that has been in evidence in the United Kingdom since the 1970s.[12] Higher-education funding in the United Kingdom has undergone a series of changes over recent decades, from an arm's-length system whereby government handed over a large sum of money to the University Grants Committee, which then disbursed it to universities, to the very different (but still largely taxpayer-supported) framework that exists today. The causes of this change have been political demands for relevance to growth and skills and a linked concern with tax-payer accountability. Government funding priorities have shifted over time in favor of the STEM subjects and against the arts, humanities, and social sciences in light of the central government's views about the importance of different subjects to economic growth. As a consequence of these changes, there has been an erosion of provision in the arts and humanities. Funding cuts in the 1980s led to the closure of numerous departments, including departments of philosophy, and more recently provision in philosophy has been threatened at Liverpool and Keele and withdrawn at Middlesex and Greenwich. One university, the University of East London, responded to financial pressures by announcing the closure of all of its arts programs. The teaching of modern languages has been particularly hard hit, with many universities abandoning these subjects entirely.

Responses by academics and their defenders to these pressures and changes have essentially been twofold. First, there have been complaints that this focus on the economic benefits of universities is absurdly narrow and that policy should also take account of the intrinsic value of research and scholarship, independent of its wider social benefit. These kinds of arguments have not been generally well received by governments, which tend to regard them as a species of special pleading by academics. If the liberal justification argument has merit, then governments have a point: again, why should taxpayers continue to fund research into, say, medieval French poetry on the grounds of its intrinsic value when it is something that many of them do not, in fact, value? In any case, many activities have intrinsic value but are not deemed worthy of state support or a place in the curriculum. Second, there have been arguments to the effect that, despite ap-pearances, the arts and humanities do provide a direct economic benefit and that the concentration on STEM subjects is therefore misguided.[13] Many of these economic counterarguments have some validity. Academics in the arts, humanities, and social sciences can point to the fact that in an economy that has moved from manufacturing to the service sector over recent decades, the skills they impart to their students have a real economic payoff, whereas government support for engineering and mathematics has led to a surplus of graduates in those fields who often do not secure jobs in manufacturing. However, just as in the United States, whilst academics are keen to stress the skills benefits of their disciplines, they show very little interest either in looking to see exactly how those skills might best be developed or in focusing directly on their development.[14] The indirect effects of, say, medieval poetry on transferable skills look like a thin and ex post facto justification for the discipline—after all, some other method or area of study might develop the same skills more effectively.

However questionable these narrowly economic arguments are, however, there is a deeper reason that we should worry about their applicability. This is that the economic argument, though presented as an acceptable one under the framework of liberal justification, actually hides some deep-seated biases that liberals should be concerned about, perhaps particularly in the context of higher education. Because of these biases, standard models of growth cannot fully supply the kind of neutral metric for policy decision making that liberal justification requires. Although it is well within the bounds of acceptable liberal justification to advance arguments based on the well-being of citizens, there is no good reason to confuse these considerations of well-being—either individually or collectively—with financial benefit, narrowly understood. The well-being of individuals is plausibly linked not only to the amount of money they earn, but also to other matters, such as the free time they have at their disposal for looking after themselves or others, for pursuing other interests including nonremunerated work, for leisure, and so forth. It is also linked to the quality of the natural and social environment, so that a society in which everyone has more money in an environment marked by increased pollution and loss of species diversity, or where there are increased levels of crime, or where it is unsafe to let children ride bicycles on the street may well be a society where people are worse off in their real standard of life, despite their greater monetary wealth. Nor is it enough to leave these questions entirely to be the outcome of individual choices, because the natural and social environment and the factors that affect people's decisions to work longer hours or not form part of the background against which individual choices are made. Liberal justification therefore has to be concerned not only with the choices people make, but also with how the menu from which choices are made gets to be written, a matter which is to a large extent subject to political decision.

Two matters in particular merit attention. The first is that there are many good reasons to think that the growth model as it has been traditionally understood will not continue to provide increases in real well-being but, rather, that the pursuit of business-as-usual growth policies both will result in catastrophic environmental harm in the fairly near future and will not be economically sustainable. The most prominent reason for this is, of course, climate change, which threatens to make much of the planet unlivable and also to inflict serious long-term economic damage.[15] Economies based on the need to extract hydrocarbons and other minerals, such as metals, will also start to struggle as these resources become progressively scarcer and rise to higher and higher prices. The second question is that the growth model as currently pursued has not, in fact, provided growth and prosperity for many citizens even of advanced countries, nor has it provided enough people with desirable and fulfilling jobs. Societies such as the United States may have become wealthier on average, but that average hides a remarkable growth in inequality of wealth and income and static or declining real standards of life for many people. Historically, the standard growth model may have been a good proxy for judging changes in real well-being. But its neglect of environmental externalities and domestic labor and its bias against leisure time means it now falls short of what we need.

There is therefore a pressing need on both environmental and social grounds for thinking about how to decouple real well-being from continual GDP growth. This is a multidisciplinary task. Part of it involves thinking about new economic models, and part of it involves philosophical reflection on the meaning of prosperity and well-being. In this latter respect the work of Amartya Sen and Martha Nussbaum in elaborating the capability model has been of great value.[16] If the economic models that we eventually adopt involve many people spending less of their time in paid employment than they do now, that also provides us with reasons to refocus our educational effort away from an almost exclusive focus on training people for jobs and toward giving them the resources that will enable them to make the best of the whole of their time. In both the elaboration of a more sophisticated understanding of well-being and in providing individuals with the cultural materials to secure it, higher education, and the arts and humanities in particular, have an indispensable role to play. Of course, these are hard or even impossible messages for political leaders to address whilst we are still living in the aftermath of the 2008 financial crash and at a time when a renewal or deepening of that crisis seems very likely. In such an atmosphere, the options seem limited to ones of ever greater austerity, with the poorest hit hardest, and a renewal of economic growth in order to provide jobs. But those limited political options do not exhaust what should be up for discussion in a liberal state, particularly if environmental and social realities will soon reassert themselves.[17]

Democratic Citizenship and the Humanities

Arguments that focus on economic and similar benefits meet the test of liberal justification in principle because they provide a demonstrable connection to the material well-being of citizens. Since all citizens are, on this account, presumed either to benefit from or, at least, not to be harmed by the supply of additional resources with which to pursue their individual plans and projects for life, we have arguments that everyone seems to have good reason to accept, even if, as actually put, they are often incomplete or misleading because of their inattention to other aspects of life. People who care about the arts and humanities, however, are likely to find the economic arguments frustrating and uncomfortable, even when they believe they have merit. Shakespeare may attract visitors to Stratford-upon-Avon and the Globe and generally boost the British economy through his effects on the tourism and publishing industries, but teachers of English literature will undoubtedly feel that this benefit, though real, is far too disconnected from the reasons that their passion warrants interest and support. If straightforward arguments of cultural and literary superiority are unavailable, however, because they cannot be shared by our fellow citizens, there nevertheless exists an attractive alternative line of justification rooted in the moral and political effects of literature and art. Justifications of this type have to be somewhat indirect, because some moral claims are impermissibly perfectionist for liberal justification; but arguments that center on the power of the arts and humanities to foster our capacities as citizens of a democratic society, and, in particular, on our abilities to act justly toward one another, look acceptable in form.[18]

Thoughts along such lines have recently been advanced by Martha Nussbaum in her book *Not for Profit*. She argues that the arts and humanities have an essential role to play in a democracy because they foster moral capacities that are essential to citizens living in relations of justice together. Specifically, she argues that the arts and humanities, by developing empathy and the ability to imagine the life of someone else, enable us to overcome divisions among humanity that foster violence, racism, and injustice. Being able to see the world from the perspective of another person who does not share our circumstances or culture, for example, is essential to being able to act with fairness and justice, and to making it possible for us to moderate our demands for self-advancement in the name of a proper recognition of the personhood and interests of strangers. I agree with Nussbaum that it is necessary for individuals to acquire the capacity to act justly toward others if we are to have a stable, just, and democratic society. I am more skeptical about her arguments that the academic study of the humanities is required for this.

An initial difficulty in evaluating Nussbaum's position comes from the variety of claims that she makes. These are often not just about higher education, but about education more generally. Since the arts and humanities are present in the curricula at all levels of the education system and also form part of the research mission of universities, an argument could be made for an important role for the humanities within education that is nevertheless compatible with the ending of all tertiary-level activity except teacher training. However, this is not her view. Instead, she argues that for democracies to be healthy, humanities education must be provided at all levels, including to students whose primary field of study is within the STEM subjects or who are pursuing business or vocational qualifications. In other words, she argues for the vital role of something like the U.S. liberal arts model. Further, she argues not just for the provision of the humanities at all these different levels and to these various recipients, but for a specific kind of pedagogy—the Socratic method—as being the key to their effective teaching. It is sometimes difficult to work out, for some feature of educational provision, whether Nussbaum thinks that particular feature is necessary for the formation of democratic citizens or merely desirable.[19]

Is it necessary that citizens, in order to acquire the democratic virtues, be exposed to the arts? And does this require that the arts form part of the curriculum? My answer here has two parts. The first is to note the pervasive place of the arts in life both historically and today, quite independently of the formal educational system. Given this, it seems likely or even certain that the arts would continue to be practiced and that humans would continue to be exposed to them whether or not we taught them explicitly in schools. The second is to draw attention, from a democratic perspective, to a grave danger in Nussbaum's stance: she risks implying that those of our fellow citizens who lack instruction in the arts and humanities to whatever degree she thinks necessary will also therefore lack the moral qualities required for them to function as full members of a democratic society.

Access to and participation in the arts has a history that predates formal educational systems and has been to a large extent conducted outside of and sometimes in conflict with such systems. Indeed, the pervasiveness of art, music, and storytelling in all human cultures suggests that we are looking at a very basic human need and drive that will continue whether or not educators and governments find a formal place for it. Indeed, whole art forms—perhaps jazz would be a good example—have been created and developed by people who are at the margins of the official educational system. Folk traditions of storytelling and song, often continued by illiterate people in many countries, ensure that narratives, often of vast complexity, are part of the common heritage of humankind. Very often we find that the official academy privileged in *Not for Profit* as the essential disseminator of cultural sensibility is the very last institution to recognize the nature and value of new artistic, literary, and musical developments, clinging to archaic models of what counts as art and literature when the real changes are happening elsewhere. If the creative aspects of culture often happen outside the academy, this is also the case with its consumption. In the passage from Raymond Williams I quoted at the beginning of this essay, he notes that ours is the first civilization in history to spend more time in watching drama than in food preparation. If exposure to imagined scenarios and the lives of other people and peoples is necessary for the development of empathic imagination, surely there is more of this now, through the medium of television, than ever before.[20]

For these reasons, I incline to optimism on the first point; but my second is that pessimism has acute dangers for the philosophical democrat and for political equality. If, contrary to my hopes for folk art and television, the vast majority of the population will not get sufficient exposure to the arts and humanities outside of the formal education system, what lesson should we then draw for democracy? Our answer to this may depend on what level of instruction turns out to be necessary in order to acquire the necessary virtues. Nussbaum seems pessimistic: "If this trend [of changes in what is taught] continues, nations all over the world will soon be producing generations of useful machines, rather than complete citizens, who can think for themselves, criticize tradition, and understand the significance of another person's sufferings and achievements. The future of the world's democracies hangs in the balance."[21] Now, as I just made clear, I am much less pessimistic about the capacity of ordinary people to secure the level of exposure to the arts that Nussbaum deems necessary for empathic imagination without a program of formal instruction; but let us assume that she is correct about this, and that formal instruction is actually required for people to function as competent citizens. We already have many citizens who are lacking in formal education of all kinds. Presumably, by Nussbaum's lights, they fail to achieve a threshold of competency. If we add to their number citizens whose competence is restricted to science, engineering, and technical or vocational subjects and who lack any record of engagement with art, literature, or music, there is a substantial proportion of the population of most advanced democracies who lack the background that Nussbaum thinks necessary to function as a full member of the political community. It is not clear what ought to follow from this. Those who think that the justification for political democracy is essentially instrumental and conditional on the quality of decision making might,[22] if they agreed with Nussbaum about the background facts, think of this as informing a case either for restricting the franchise or for giving multiple votes to those who enjoy the relevant competencies.[23] Others, whose commitment to democracy is based on some right to participation flowing from political equality,[24] will be more troubled if many citizens lack the qualities necessary to make effective use of the rights they enjoy.

It is best if citizens have all the desirable cognitive and emotional attributes needed for full participation, insofar as they have the capacity to acquire them. Those capacities for critical reasoning, argument, and empathic imagination are identified by Nussbaum with the humanities. Other capacities, including statistical analysis, deductive logic, and scientific reasoning, generally are more closely associated with the sciences. If we are designing a curriculum with the aim of political participation as a key aim, but one that it must share with others—because citizens have wider interests than just politics—what the balance between these two sides should be seems to be an open question. Capacities for the kinds of cognitive engagement necessary for democracy are associated with a range of different subjects. Some of them—certainly mathematics and the natural sciences—cannot be acquired without formal instruction. In the case of the capacities distinctively fostered by the humanities, it may be, as I have argued, that a considerable amount can be picked up from the wider culture, such as television, reading, music, and so on. To the extent to which this is so, the implications for the curriculum do not necessarily favor the humanities. In addition, since both adults and children vary in their aptitude for the sciences, humanities, and education generally, there must also be worries about designing education in such a way that those whose natural bent is on "the other side" are obliged to receive instruction in the disciplines for which they feel least affinity. There has to be at least a risk that such classes are resented by their recipients, with effects very much the opposite of those Nussbaum wants to produce.

In *Not for Profit*, however, Nussbaum is a firm advocate of the broad-based U.S. system, even in tertiary education. She makes this clear in a passage where she commends the U.S. model, counsels against any attempt to water it down by distinguishing between core and non-core humanities disciplines, and holds up the example of Europe, with its tendency for students to concentrate on one or two subjects over a narrow range, as providing a mode and content of higher education ill-suited to democratic citizenship.[25] It is hard to know how we might evaluate these claims. Nussbaum's own procedure seems to be one of thinking about the ideal of democratic citizenship and the kinds of knowledge (say, of other countries and cultures) that would be necessary for its exercise. She then notes that these are more salient in the U.S. system than elsewhere. But other ways of thinking about the problem do suggest themselves. We could look at the political cultures of different countries, at their rates of participation in elections and membership of political parties, at the quality of political debate in their mass media, and at a host of similar indicators. We could then ask whether those countries, whose tertiary education system is modeled on the liberal arts, tend to do better in these dimensions than those whose students study a narrower range of subjects. I have not conducted such a survey, so I can only rely on impression and guesswork, but my current belief is that the political culture of Western Europe is not in worse shape than that of the United States. Of course, there are many complex historical reasons, going far beyond the educational system, that explain why countries have the political cultures that they do. So, noticing a lack of correlation between the features of the educational system that Nussbaum finds desirable and the political effects she prizes, her argument cannot be taken as conclusive. It may be that without a liberal arts approach the political culture of the United States would be worse than it is, and that with such an approach that of Western Europe would be improved. Similar thoughts and arguments can be deployed concerning the style of pedagogy for which Nussbaum argues (Socratic and participatory rather than passive and authoritarian). The French educational system, for example, is notably authoritarian in style at all levels, yet this does not seem to result in a marked citizenship deficit compared to the United States.

Some of the difficulties with Nussbaum's arguments, as I see them, stem from her propensity to make stronger claims than she needs. An argument defending the humanities from a politically liberal perspective need not make the case that the provision of the humanities in some form to all students at all levels is absolutely necessary if citizens are to acquire the capacities they need for democratic participation. Weaker and more defensible arguments are available, ones that can draw on the evidence she adduces. First, we can argue that exposure to the humanities at *some* level is both desirable for the formation of citizens of a liberal state and also necessary, because without such exposure it will be impossible for them to learn important facts about themselves, whether their own aptitudes are for arts, sciences, or some mix of the two. Secondly, a social version of Nussbaum's argument is surely more plausible than the one she puts. It may not be necessary to democracy that everyone receive an education in the humanities, but it is surely necessary that arguments derived from the humanities—from art, literature, and history—find a place within the political process. If we think about democracy as a collaborative and social process involving a conversation among citizens where each brings his or her own particular knowledge and skills to the discussion, we can see that it is not essential that each person have the full complement of abilities and information, but rather that these are present somewhere in the system and are able to get a hearing. A democratic conversation after September 11, 2001, for example, did not require that everyone have a background in Middle Eastern politics, history, and Islamic theology, but it did require that there be some citizens with this knowledge and the capacity to inform and explain to others; it can be very hard to predict which particular specialty will turn out to be relevant.[26] From these two points, a great deal of what Nussbaum wants as a matter of practice and policy surely follows. If children are to be exposed to literature, art, and history, then they surely need to be taught by teachers, who first need to be educated. If some citizens need to be informed about the history of Islam or the Russian novel, then someone needs to educate them. If we are to have experts on those subjects to write for our mass media and communicate with their fellow citizens, then we surely need some researchers at a high level and university departments that will produce new generations of researchers, educators, and so on.

A third source of liberal justification for the humanities focuses neither on furnishing material resources to people nor on their political life as citizens of a democratic society, but on providing individuals with a range of possible modes of life and with the tools necessary critically to evaluate the life choices they might make. This sort of argument has its roots in the thought of John Stuart Mill: the humanities provide material for "experiments in living."[27] On this account, the humanities are seen not, as they are in conservative elitist defenses of them, as being the guardians of objective value, but rather as preserving the diversity of possible ways of living in the face of societal (and especially market) pressures to conformity. In Mill's own work, these ideas are given a perfectionist spin through their connection to a rather substantive conception of autonomy, but it is perfectly possible to recast them in Rawlsian terms. In *Political Liberalism*, Rawls attributes to citizens an interest in and a capacity for reflection on the nature of the good life and the ability to form, revise, and pursue a conception of the good. Citizens with such an interest have a related interest in having material to work with, and art, literature, and history can provide individuals with sources of inspiration and reflection concerning what their aims in life should be.[28] Similarly to the "democratic citizenship" case for the humanities, this justification, focused on providing citizens with adequate resources to make and reflect on their life choices, has implications for the curriculum to the extent to which it is the case that citizens will otherwise lack access to essential cognitive resources. Similarly to that argument, citizens also can benefit from other nonhumanities education (mathematics and the natural sciences) in evaluating their own choices, but it seems plausible that the humanities, in depicting the history and imaginative choices involved in other lives, can have a special role to play in helping people to get a perspective on their own.

The Humanities as an Essential Source of Knowledge

The well-being of citizens generally, the associative needs of democratic polities, and the interest citizens have in forming and revising their conceptions of the good give us reasons to support the arts and humanities as fields of study and inquiry, reasons that can meet the test of liberal justification. Some will think, though, that there is something unsatisfactory about these justifications. They may pass the liberal justification test, but they also have the flavor of desperate rationalizations of practices developed for other reasons and in different times. The reasons the traditional university curriculum in the arts and humanities has the shape that it does have very little to do with its real usefulness for economic development and not much to do with a liberal and democratic ideal of citizenship.[29] Rather, they are often connected to ancient religious affiliations and to conceptions of the kinds of knowledge appropriate to the exercise of aristocratic virtue. Now that those historical causes and justifications of a set of institutions have fallen away, as happens so often in human life, people look around for new justifying reasons.

However, there may still be another justification that passes muster. In this final section, I shall concentrate on a more methodological and perspective-based justification in support of the humanities as being part of the scientific enterprise broadly conceived. This does not entirely vindicate the humanities as such, but it puts them under the protective canopy of a wider set of practices that are much less politically and socially controversial. The scientific enterprise in this broad sense, having to do with the discovery of knowledge about the world, is not entirely without critics, since skeptics occasionally doubt the usefulness of pure science and mathematics, but still stands less exposed than the humanities. This final source of justification is that (a) the human world, the world of human experience, is a bona fide part of the world, to be equally considered as those parts of the world studied by the natural sciences, and (b) its study requires methods of understanding and interpretation developed by and characteristic of the humanities. This has two aspects. First, because the methodologies of the humanities discover genuine truths about aspects of the world that are invisible or impenetrable to the natural sciences, the humanities are operating in parallel with the natural sciences. Secondly, for some objects of study the humanities provide us with a perspective that is complementary to that of the natural sciences.

The claim that the humanities and the human sciences more generally give us access to some truths about our human world that the natural sciences cannot provide is an old one, associated with Vico and with Dilthey's distinction between the *Geisteswissenschaften* and the *Naturwissenschaften* and with the contrasting methods of *verstehen* and *erklären*. Some versions of this thesis put it in a very strong form, claiming that lived human reality, saturated as it is with meaning, is knowable only by interpretation.[30] On this strong view, only subjects who themselves interpret subjects can grasp the inner semantic connections and contrasts among the various elements of a text or an artwork and the wider social and cultural reality of which it forms a part. Only humans with interpretative skill can understand the significance of particular actions and gestures within a social complex. These strong versions deny, in principle, that it is ever possible to understand society using the methods of the natural sciences. That seems much too strong. In psychology, sociology, economics, and other disciplines in the social sciences, there is surely a role for the observation of regularities, for experiment, and for new perspectives on our world that show how humanistic understanding can mislead us. A more moderate thesis seems in order, one that allows for humanistic methods and those of the natural sciences to be complementary in understanding the human world. In practice, we are unable to understand that world, and especially the historical elements of it, without drawing on our capacities for empathy, grasping meaning, and imaginative understanding. If we believe, for example, that a proper understanding of who we are and the societies in which we now live depends, to some extent, on grasping the historical origins of those societies, then we will also believe that humanistic understanding is an essential component of the broad knowledge-gathering enterprise.

We need not confine ourselves, however, to the idea that the humanities have a role to play in the acquisition of knowledge for its own sake. The humanities can complement the applied sciences, medicine, and engineering precisely because of their sensitivity to the perspective of the subject and her lived experience. Let me give two examples of this, the first from architecture and the second from medicine.

The prestige of the natural sciences in the early and middle parts of the twentieth century led to the widespread adoption of an engineering perspective in fields such as architecture and urban design. However, this focus on inputs and outputs and on designing "machines for living" based on an abstract specification of human need turned out to be disastrous in human terms. It turned out that the subjective, and indeed aesthetic, experience of people was essential for them to live in anything like well-functioning communities.[31]

A second illustration of this complementary "hard" science and human experience is the emerging field of medical humanities, a group of related interdisciplinary fields of study linking the humanities (including literature, philosophy, ethics, history, religion, anthropology, cultural studies, psychology, sociology, drama, film, and visual and performing arts) and their application to medicine. Their aim is to understand the relationship between medicine and these fields and to exploit the insights they can provide into medical education and practice. The medical humanities are an important complement to the enormous body of natural-scientific information that forms the major part of medical training. Obviously medical practitioners have to acquire and master that basic scientific knowledge, but they also work in what is primarily a person-centered discipline. To prevent and alleviate the suffering of individuals, physicians must understand it not only from a scientific point of view, but also from the perspective of the patient. The medical humanities aim to explore and develop the humanistic side of medicine through literature, arts, and history. They also provide doctors with helpful perspectives on scientific knowledge of which they have hitherto been largely passive consumers by enabling them to cast a critical gaze on this knowledge and by considering the changing social, anthropological, and historical contexts of the production of medical knowledge and reflecting philosophically on its nature and significance. The medical humanities aim to deepen our understanding of the relationship between medicine as a science and medicine as a humanistic practice and thus to enrich the education and understanding of our doctors.[32]

An emphasis on the humanities' methodological distinctiveness; on the membership in them of science, broadly conceived; on the theoretical complement to other parts of the scientific enterprise; and on the humanities' practical benefits can go a long way toward vindicating the whole area of inquiry against its more Gradgrindian critics. What it does not necessarily do is leave intact the humanities as they are currently conceived and divided. The traditional divisions within humanities scholarship are not necessarily the most conducive either to the scientific enterprise or to the broader instrumental goals I have written about here. That said, the historic disciplinary map has produced communities of scholarship with formidable records of collective achievement. Though academic managers often feel the impulse to break down disciplinary boundaries, there is always the danger that in doing so they are destroying valuable networks for collaboration and research that have evolved over time, and that new divisions will not work so well in practice.

Conclusion

The conclusion I should wish to reach is that the humanities need to be much less defensive than they have been. Even if we adopt a relatively austere principle of justification and eschew arguments that depend on the special civilizational value of the humanities, there are sufficient resources available, within public and political reason, to mount a defense for the place of these subjects within the academy. The humanities can help us see that the economic-growth arguments beloved by politicians, but ultimately threatening to both our well-being and that of the planet, can be challenged or supplemented by other considerations bearing on the ability of citizens to form, revise, and pursue their aims. Though the democratic-citizenship case put forth by Martha Nussbaum proved to claim a little too much, the humanities have an essential contribution to make to the democratic conversation. We do not need for all citizens to be educated in the humanities in order to play their part, but we do need the humanities to contribute to public debate and discussion in order to make all citizens aware of the full range of values and considerations bearing on public issues. Finally, the humanities have an important role to play in society more generally, both in providing distinctive forms of knowledge alongside the natural sciences and as being, in important ways, complementary to them.

Bibliography

Arneson, Richard. 2000. "Rawls versus Utilitarianism in the Light of Political Liberalism." In The Idea of Political Liberalism: Essays on Rawls, edited by Victoria Davion and Clark Wolf. Lanham, MD: Rowman & Littlefield.
———. 2004. "Democracy Is Not Intrinsically Just." In Justice and Democracy: Essays for

Brian Barry, edited by Robert E. Goodin, Carole Pateman, and Keith Dowding. Cambridge: Cambridge University Press.

Bate, Jonathan, ed. 2001. The Public Value of the Humanities. London: Bloomsbury.

Bertram, Christopher. 1997. "Political Justification, Theoretical Complexity, and Democratic Community." Ethics 107, no. 1: 563–83.

Bok, Derek. 2006. Our Underachieving Colleges: A Candid Look at How Much Students Learn and Why They Should Be Learning More. Princeton, NJ: Princeton University Press.

Brand, Stewart. 1994. How Buildings Learn: What Happens After They're Built. New York: Penguin.

Brighouse, Harry. 1996. "Egalitarianism and Equal Availability of Political Influence." Journal of Political Philosophy 4, no. 2: 118–41.

Browne, John, Michael Barber, Diane Coyle, David Eastwood, Julia King, Rajay Naik, and Peter Sands. 2010. Securing a Sustainable Future for Higher Education in England. https://www.gov.uk/government/uploads/system/uploads/attachment_data/file/31999/10-1208-securing-sustainable-higher-education-browne-report.pdf.

Carel, Havi. 2008. Illness: The Cry of the Flesh. Stocksfield: Acumen.

Collini, Stefan. 2011. "From Robbins to McKinsey." London Review of Books 33, no. 16 (August): 9–14.

———. 2012. What Are Universities For? London: Penguin.

Jackson, Tim. 2009. Prosperity without Growth: Economics for a Finite Planet. London: Earthscan.

Jacobs, Jane. 1961. The Death and Life of Great American Cities. New York: Vintage Books.

Levitt, Ruth, Barbara Janta, Alaa Shehabi, Daniel Jones, and Elizabeth Valentini. 2009. Language Matters: The Supply of and Demand for UK Born and Educated Academic Researchers with Skills in Languages Other than English. Santa Monica, CA: Rand Europe for the British Academy.

MacDonald, Graham, and Philip Pettit. 1981. Semantics and Social Science. London: Routledge.

Mill, John Stuart. 1975. "Considerations on Representative Government." In Three Essays, edited by Richard Wollheim. Oxford: Oxford University Press.

———. 1982. On Liberty. Edited by Gertrude Himmelfarb. Harmondsworth: Penguin.

Nussbaum, Martha C. 2000. Women and Human Development: The Capabilities Approach. Cambridge: Cambridge University Press.

———. 2010. Not for Profit: Why Democracy Needs the Humanities. Princeton, NJ: Princeton University Press.

Rawls, John. 1993. Political Liberalism. New York: Columbia University Press.

———. 1999. "The Idea of Public Reason Revisited." In Collected Papers, edited by Samuel Freeman. Cambridge, MA: Harvard University Press.

Raz, Joseph. 1986. The Morality of Freedom. Oxford: Oxford University Press.

Schor, Juliet B. 2010. Plenitude: The New Economics of True Wealth. New York: Penguin.

Scott, James C. 1998. Seeing like a State: How Certain Schemes to Improve the Human Condition Have Failed. New Haven, CT: Yale University Press.

Sen, Amartya. 1999. Development as Freedom. Oxford: Oxford University Press.

Stern, Nicholas. 2007. The Economics of Climate Change: The Stern Review. Cambridge: Cambridge University Press.

Stout, Jeffrey. 2004. Democracy and Tradition. Princeton, NJ: Princeton University Press.

Taylor, Charles. 1971. "Interpretation and the Sciences of Man." Review of Metaphysics 25, no. 3: 1–45.

Waldron, Jeremy. 1987. "Theoretical Foundations of Liberalism." *Philosophical Quarterly* 37, no. 47: 127–50.

Williams, Raymond. 1974. *Television: Technology and Cultural Form.* London: Fontana.

Notes

I would like to thank participants in the Spencer Foundation conference Values in Higher Education at Northwestern University and at a Spencer workshop held in preparation for that occasion. Megan Blomfield, Harry Brighouse, Ann Cudd, Anthony Laden, Mike McPherson, and Grace Roosevelt provided me with written comments that have been most useful in revising the text. Alexander Bird and Havi Carel also provided me with useful research materials.

1. A recent collection of papers expressive of this anxiety is Bate (2001); see also Collini (2012).
2. Bok (2006), 283.
3. Williams (1974), 56.
4. Nussbaum (2010).
5. Perfectionist liberals, such as Joseph Raz (see Raz 1986); and consequentialist ones, like Richard Arneson (see Arneson 2000).
6. See Waldron (1987). The general antiperfectionist account of justification that I discuss in this section draws on, e.g., Rawls (1993), among many other sources.
7. I explore some difficulties with securing such acceptance in Bertram (1997).
8. For a surprising argument to this effect, see John Rawls's discussion of the debate between James Madison and Patrick Henry in Rawls (1999), 602.
9. Collini (2011), included in Collini (2012).
10. Speech by Barack Obama on education, March 10, 2009. Another alarming passage in the speech is discussed in Nussbaum (2010), 138.
11. In her contribution to this volume, Erin Kelly distinguishes the business, economic-development, and scholarcentric models of the university. The now-dominant view in the United Kingdom represents an amalgam of the first two of these.
12. Browne, Barber, Coyle, Eastwood, King, Naik, and Sands (2010).
13. See, e.g., Levitt, Janta, Shehabi, Jones, and Valentini (2009).
14. On this, for the United States, see Bok (2006), chapter 11.
15. That climate change unaddressed will do serious economic harm is the central contention of the Stern report; see Stern (2007).
16. See, among very many other works, Sen (1999) and Nussbaum (2000).
17. In these last three paragraphs I've been influenced particularly by Jackson (2009) and Schor (2010).
18. Some readers may worry at this point that the requirement that citizens abstain from promoting their favored policy on impermissibly perfectionist grounds could mask a set of hypocritical and deceptive practices whereby arguments are advanced in one form but secretly motivated by unshareable "real" reasons; see, e.g., Stout (2004), chapter 3, for this kind of concern. But it seems to me that this anxiety that citizens might argue in bad faith is one that fails to give sufficient weight to the idea that giving reasons to one's fellow citizens that they can reasonably be expected to endorse is itself a moral reason that people should normally attach trumping importance to.
19. There are more questions about the connection between the acquisition of culture and democratic citizenship and empathic imagination, which I shall note but not

probe further. These concern Nussbaum's claims that such exposure has the positive benefits she describes, claims that rest, in the book at least, on psychoanalytic and pedagogical literature rather than on rigorous empirical investigation. Without such investigation, however, we are very much in the realm of anecdote; and, however plausible the idea, competing anecdotes and narratives can always be deployed. The members of the highly cultivated and humanistically educated German officer class of the 1930s and '40s, for example, do not appear to have been imbued with the virtues of democratic citizenship and empathic imagination to any great degree, and they remind us that a sense of cultural superiority can also ground feelings of contempt, hatred, or revulsion toward the "other," as Nussbaum herself is often keen to emphasize. One could also, in the light of recent psychological studies, question the importance she places on qualities of character and moral dispositions as features of the person in a democratic society. For example, one school of thought claims that character is less important to behavior than circumstance, but that we are psychologically predisposed—wrongly—to prefer character-based explanations. (Such an allegedly mistaken predisposition is at the core of the novelist's art.) If such a view were right and conventional wisdom were mistaken, then it would undermine the case for focusing on individual dispositions as necessary for the functioning of a democratic society in favor of other determinants of behavior, such as institutional design. But for the sake of argument I grant Nussbaum's commitments about both the importance of character and the beneficial effects of exposure to art and literature on empathic imagination and prosocial dispositions.

20. This is not to deny that the best teaching in the humanities can provide students with a critical take on mass culture that can enhance democracy. But I am skeptical about how much actual teaching in the humanities meets this threshold and relatively optimistic about the capacity of ordinary people to escape the condition of merely passive consumption. For some worries about how fostering a critical attitude in students can actually foster a shallow dismissiveness, see Kyla Ebels-Duggan's contribution to this volume.

21. Nussbaum (2010), 2.

22. E.g., Arneson (2004).

23. Very much on the model of chapter 8 in Mill (1975).

24. For one example of such a view, see Brighouse (1996).

25. Nussbaum (2010), 125–28.

26. Very much to the point is the following observation from Jonathan Bate: "In the light of the recent historical developments for which '9/11' can serve as shorthand, it was perhaps unfortunate that the swingeing funding cuts to higher education [in the United Kingdom] in the early 1980s fell with particular severity on supposedly marginal areas of the humanities such as Islamic studies." "Introduction," Bate (2001), 2.

27. Mill (1982), chapter 3.

28. Rawls himself seems unnecessarily hesitant on this point, conceding in "The Priority of Right and Ideas of the Good" that the reasonable requirements of children's education may approximate those promoted by the more comprehensive liberalisms, but referring to this with "regret." Rawls (1993), 199–200.

29. For some discussion of the evolution of the curriculum in the United States, see Bok (2006), chapter 1.

30. For one classic argument to this effect, see Taylor (1971); for critical discussion, see MacDonald and Pettit (1981).

31. The key text for this dispute is, of course, Jacobs (1961); but see also Brand (1994);

and the discussion of Le Corbusier in Scott (1998), chapter 4, and Scott's discussion of practical knowledge, chapter 9.

32. I have been assisted in this paragraph by Alexander Bird, who has set up a pioneering program in the medical humanities at the University of Bristol. A good particular example of this engagement between the humanities and medical science is Carel (2008), a remarkable book that draws on the author's own life. A philosopher trained in the methods of phenomenology, Carel was diagnosed with a serious and debilitating condition with a prognosis of a much shortened life. During Carel's diagnosis and treatment, she was struck by the detached, clinical, and "scientific" approach of her doctors, which seemed to her to miss a vitally important aspect of what was going on: namely, what it is like for the patient. Drawing on the work of Merleau-Ponty, Carel writes of the importance of augmenting physiological description and clinical intervention with an account of the first-person perspective of the patient as a mode of experience and interaction with the world and other people. Recently she has been working to show how clinical practice and patient care can be improved by taking into account of the embodied nature of the patient's experience.

FOUR

Academic Friendship

PAUL WEITHMAN

In this essay, I offer some philosophically informed reflection on the aims of college and university teaching. In doing so, I shall draw on my own experience, which is that of teaching philosophy at a selective private university that is also religious. Although my experience is not typical of my profession, I hope that what I have to say will resonate with all college and university teachers who are committed to giving their students a good education.

I begin by observing that the relationship between teachers and students is a partnership. When that relationship flourishes, the partnership becomes a kind of friendship I shall refer to as "academic friendship." While other kinds of academic friendships can develop between an advisor and advisees or between a professor and teaching assistants, the academic friendship that I shall discuss is that which develops between a professor and undergraduate students in his or her class.

In the first section I explore what kind of relationship such an academic friendship can be. It is often said that education should aim at making students autonomous. In the second section however, I argue that while autonomy is a worthy goal of higher education, it is not sufficient. In the third section I discuss qualities of mind other than those constitutive of autonomy that college and university education should try to encourage. In the fourth section I draw on the first section's treatment of academic friendship to describe how those qualities might be encouraged. I close by considering the claim that the conception of education I have sketched is objectionably elitist.

I

Academic friendship, as I understand it, is a good in the lives of students and teachers that deserves to be chosen for its own sake; yet it also has ends beyond itself that help to give the friendship its point. One is an end at which all parties to the friendship should aim: learning. Another is an end that it is the special responsibility of the teacher to have in view: the development in his or her students of certain qualities of mind that—it is hoped—they will continue to exercise at least episodically after their experience with that teacher ends. The classic discussion of friendship in the philosophical literature is Aristotle's. It will be useful to see where academic friendship fits into the schema that Aristotle developed.

Aristotle famously distinguished true friendships from two other kinds of friendships, those founded on pleasure and those based on utility.[1] His example of the third kind is the friendship that develops between, for example, business associates, each of whom enters into the partnership for his or her own benefit.[2] In the contemporary world of higher education, the partnership between teachers and students might seem to fit most comfortably into this third category.

It is commonly remarked that higher education has become increasingly commodified, meaning in part that learning is treated more and more—by administrators, faculty, and students—as a product whose value is strictly instrumental and determined by market forces. One of the ways commodification shows itself is in the expectations that students and faculty bring to their relationship. When education is commodified, students regard themselves as customers who are entitled to satisfaction with a product for which they have paid—a product provided by a professor who feels obliged to cater to demand and taste for fear of receiving negative evaluations from consumers. Under those circumstances, any friendship that develops between teachers and students is likely to fall into Aristotle's third category.

But the treatment of education as a commodity that must be tailored to satisfy student demand is a mistake. The mistake consists, at least in part, in seriously misunderstanding how the goods of a classroom education are to be identified and conveyed. They are not to be identified by consulting student demand, since students have at best an imperfect knowledge of what facts and skills they need to master. And those facts and skills are not to be conveyed in ways that cater to students' tastes, since students may not bring to the classroom a taste for the rigor that mastery of those facts and skills requires. The academic friendship that develops when education is commodified has inherent limits. After all, the friendship depends upon parties to it satisfying one another's expectations of a relationship that is beneficial as judged by the desires brought to the partnership. I have said that the partnership between professors and students has a point beyond itself at which the professor should aim, and that that point is encouraging in students certain qualities of mind. I shall contend later that among those qualities of mind is a taste for intellectually demanding material. If that is right, then the professor should try to make his or her partnership with students formative: he or she should strive to form students' intellectual tastes. Professors cannot do that if—under threat of adverse student evaluations, for example[3]—they take commodification to its logical conclusion, thus treating students' tastes as given and treating professors' pedagogical task as that of catering to them.[4]

The friendship that should develop between teachers and students has some affinities to the best form of a kind of friendship that Aristotle mentions in passing: the friendship that can develop among fellow travelers. This relationship may seem an unpromising model for the partnership between teachers and students, since Aristotle brings it up to show how relationships can break down over disagreements about common expenses and to exemplify what he seems to regard as attenuated uses of the word *friend*.[5] In fact, the relationship between fellow travelers can be an approximation, albeit a limited one, of true friendship. It is this possibility that I want briefly to explore.

In true friendship, Aristotle says, the partners in the friendship recognize one another's good character. They spend time together in activities in which they develop and exercise the virtues that make their characters good. When partners engage in such activities over time, and when the engagement deepens their appreciation for each other's good character, they develop affection for each other that itself helps to sustain the friendship.[6] In perfect friendships, this affection is especially deep. Each develops the kind of affection for the other that he or she has for him- or herself. That is why Aristotle speaks of a true friend as "another self."[7]

A friendship that develops among fellow travelers is not a perfect one—at least, not if the trip is reasonably short and the further development of the friendship is arrested by the end of the journey. It can, however, have elements of true friendship. Fellow travelers can come to recognize one another's generosity and forbearance, their curiosity about new peoples and places, and their dedication to learning more about the sites to which their travels take them. They can spend time together in activities in which they exercise and further develop these qualities of character. Travel can, of course, be informative and broadening. When it is, travelers exercise their virtues of curiosity and openness in the individual and joint realization of goods that are both instrumentally and intrinsically valuable. Some of the affection characteristic of friendship can develop through mutual aid in coping with the challenges and inconveniences of travel. But it can also develop through the deepened acquaintance brought about by passing time together and, more important, by the shared experience of discovery.

Like the partnership between fellow travelers, that between students and professors does not have the potential for perfect friendship. Parties to the educational partnership, like fellow travelers, know that their time together does not extend into the indefinite future—that it will end with the conclusion of the quarter or the semester, as travelers know theirs will end with the conclusion of their trip. But that partnership can still exhibit some of the characteristics of true friendship, and for some of the same reasons that a partnership between fellow travelers can. When education goes well, professors and students learn from one another. Professors deepen their knowledge of curricular material by teaching it, and they learn how effectively to adapt their presentations of that material to successive generations of students with different sets of intellectual and cultural reference points. Students, of course, are expected to master the material presented to them and to ask questions that deepen their own understanding. Thus, like the activities of travel when a trip goes well, the activities constitutive of education are—when they go well—informative and broadening. And, as with travel, the goods realized in those activities are intrinsically as well as instrumentally valuable.

Teaching and learning draw on qualities of character, about which I shall say more shortly, that professors and students exercise in the pursuit and attainment of those goods. As in travel, so in education, some of those qualities are displayed in mutual aid. Those on the same trip can thus serve as one another's allies against its difficulties. At least in the humanities, where even someone who has taught the same material for many years can still arrive at a deeper understanding of it, students and professors can serve as allies against the difficulty of academic material. Their appreciation of one another's character, of what each brings to the educational enterprise, of their shared concern for its success and of the shared joy of discovery, can all lead to bonds of friendly affection. The development of the appropriate kind of friendship between professors and students is one of the joys of teaching. The friendship itself is a good in the lives of both teachers and students and can heighten commitment to the educational enterprise on both sides.

Another feature of the educational partnership that keeps it from being a perfect friendship is that it lacks the equality that Aristotle thought necessary for such a friendship.[8] One inequality is an inequality of emotional, social, and intellectual development; another is an inequality of power. These differences imply that there are some activities that parties to the friendship will not want to share, and also some that it would be inappropriate for them to share. The fact that so much will not and ought not be shared limits the depth and intensity the friendship can reach. But the inequalities that account for those limits also give the friendship its point. It is because of students' stage in their intellectual development, and their interest in developing further through education, that they enter into a partnership with their teachers by putting themselves under their teachers' authority and guidance. Teachers enter into it by assuming responsibility for developing their students. Thus, the friendship that can emerge between them is like that among fellow travelers—but in which one of the travelers has the job of planning the journey for the education of his or her companions so that they develop in ways that they continue to draw on after their discoveries have been made and their journey ends.

I have explored the possibility of a kind of friendship between professors and students because I believe it sheds light on the character and aims of the partnership between professors and students. Desirable qualities loom large in Aristotle's treatment of friendship, and the development that professors are responsible for stimulating in their students is in part the development of certain desirable qualities of mind. According to Aristotle, friends recognize and are drawn to one another's good qualities. The affection born of this mutual recognition sustains commitment to the joint activities in which those qualities are exercised and further developed. This development on students' part is the point of the partnership between professors and students. I want to suggest that one way professors should contribute to its attainment is by modeling the qualities of mind we want our students to acquire. We should do so in hopes that as a result of our academic friendship with them, they will be drawn to those qualities and will want to exercise them themselves. In the next section, I shall begin to identify those qualities and say what is desirable about them.

II

It is often said that formal education should be education for autonomy, a claim defended by political, instrumental, and perfectionist arguments. According to the political argument, education should foster the qualities of mind needed for liberal democratic citizenship and autonomy—or, more precisely, the qualities whose exercise makes for autonomy. According to the instrumental argument, education for autonomy helps students to realize their interest in leading a good life;[9] according to the perfectionist argument, students should be educated for autonomy because education should foster the qualities needed to lead a good life, and autonomy is one of those qualities.

The political and instrumental arguments have obvious advantages if what is wanted are arguments that can publicly justify an education for autonomy. Such arguments would have to show that education for autonomy serves legitimate public purposes. The political and instrumental arguments promise to do that, while the perfectionist argument—appealing as it does to claims about the good life—seems not to.[10] I believe that many of us who teach at colleges and universities—whether or not we have the philosophical vocabulary to say it—are perfectionists about autonomy. We think autonomy is partially constitutive of a good life and choice-worthy as an end in itself. If I was right to suggest at the end of the previous section that professors can and should model the qualities we want our students to acquire, then it follows that we should model autonomy.

What is an education for autonomy? I take its advocates to mean that one of the goals of formal education should be to encourage students to hold their beliefs—or some important, though not necessarily large, subset of their beliefs—autonomously.

What is it to hold beliefs autonomously? This is not easy to determine from the writings of those who favor education for autonomy. One of the difficulties is that, though moral philosophers have done a great deal of work on autonomy in recent decades, their work is rarely engaged by those who take autonomy to be the goal of education. As a result, it is hard to tell how the uses of the word *autonomy* in the educational literature are connected to those that are paradigmatic in practical philosophy, such as Kant's use of it to refer to giving oneself the moral law. I conjecture that the common idea is this: to act autonomously is to follow the authority of reason. To live autonomously is to follow the authority of reason in the ongoing conduct of one's life. To hold one's beliefs autonomously is to follow the authority of reason in determining what to believe about how to live or what to do. By that I take advocates of education for autonomy to mean that students should be taught to endorse those beliefs about how to live or what to do that they think enjoy the strongest rational support.

Holding one's beliefs autonomously in this sense requires the acquisition of certain concepts and skills, including some perhaps inarticulate grasp of the concepts of reasons for belief and of rational support. It also helps to be able to distinguish various kinds of rational support—such as inductive, probabilistic, and deductive—to assess degrees of support, and to recognize common fallacies. Assessing degrees of support, in turn, requires a skill that is more often described metaphorically than analyzed: that of "distancing" oneself from one's beliefs or of gaining "critical distance" from them.[11] Only when such distance is gained will the degree of confidence someone attaches to a belief reflect what he or she takes to be the strength of the evidence for it, rather than—for example—the emotional investment one may have in it because it is one's own.

Education for autonomy is generally thought to include an education in these skills.[12] Sometimes it is also thought to require education for public deliberation, so that students learn to offer reasons for their beliefs about what the polity should do and so that they learn how to support, change, modify, or compromise their views when confronted with appropriately strong counterarguments.[13] Exercising these skills is said to be compatible with holding beliefs about how to live on the basis of trust or testimony, provided one thinks—or, perhaps, one sees how—the trusted or testifying source can itself be rationally supported.

I said earlier that I think most of us who teach at colleges and universities are at least tacit perfectionists about autonomy. And so I believe most us think that seeing where reason leads, believing on its basis and recognizing its limits, enables students to realize very great intellectual values and to lead lives that are, in that important respect, intrinsically better than the alternatives. That is why, regardless of our discipline, we try to educate our students in the skills I have just described.

Why is it better to lead a life characterized by the exercise of reason and distancing? One standard answer is that such a life is better because it is, in important ways, free. For when one guides one's life by the authority of one's own reason, one is said to be living a life that is "self-governing" and therefore independent.[14] Furthermore, leading a self-governing life is thought to be incompatible with complacency, dogmatism, unquestioning trust, and blindly following the dictates of parental or religious authority in determining how to live or what to do. So a life that is independent in this way is free of the various forms of unreason that some college and university teachers think are prevalent among their students. The belief that these defects are prevalent no doubt goes some way toward explaining the emphasis on education for autonomy in recent literature in the philosophy of education.

Educating our students for autonomy presupposes that they can and will develop a desire to exercise those skills. It presupposes, in other words, that they can and will develop a desire to follow for its own sake what they take to be the authority of reason in deciding what to believe about how to live. But how they can take an interest in what reason dictates, so that they acknowledge and are therefore moved by its authority, is not at all well understood, in part because of the difficulty of saying exactly what the desire to follow the authority of reason is a desire *for*. It seems unlikely that the desire we want to encourage in our students is simply a first-order desire just to respond to what they take to be good reasons, without any accompanying higher-order desires. Since we want students to reflect on why they believe what they do, we would like them to respond to good reasons as such, under that description. But is this a desire to follow epistemic principles that reason validates? Or is it, in the first instance, a desire to be the kind of person who frees him- or herself from dogmatism and prejudice and who follows such principles?

I shall assume that the desire to follow reason's authority, and thereby to realize autonomy as understood here, either includes or is heightened by the desire to be such a person. If we are to educate students for autonomy, we have to arouse or implant that desire in them. We can model the qualities we want them to acquire by evincing openmindedness and intellectual honesty, as well as concern for evidence, clarity of reasoning, and soundness of argument. I said in the first section that our students could come to desire the qualities of mind we model for them if our partnership with them has developed into an academic friendship. An argument Samuel Scheffler has made in another connection suggests that this might happen as a result of our modeling those qualities.

In modeling the qualities of autonomy, we show that we are subject to the same authority that we expect our students to acknowledge: the authority of reason. Scheffler has argued that the experience of subjection to a common authority can give rise to a sense of solidarity among those who are thus subjected and hence to a kind of friendship among them. While Scheffler's paradigms are cases of subjection to a common authoritative person, he says that bonds of solidarity and friendship can also develop in the case of common subjection to the authority of norms:

> We must all confront the normative dimension of human experience. We all live in the shadow of norms, principles, reasons, and ideals that, rightly or wrongly, we regard as authoritative. And although our values vary, the experience of responding to normative authority—of trying to be guided by values and norms that we accept—is part of our common experience. And this too makes possible a form of solidarity—a form of solidarity that derives from the shared experience of subjection, not to a common authority figure, but to normativity or authority itself.[15]

Scheffler's argument is interesting and suggestive. While he does not say that common subjection to authority of reason as I have discussed it here creates solidarity, his argument raises the question of whether evidence of that common subjection can itself provide grounds for friendship between a professor and his or her students.

We might think that it can, at least when the students first arrive in college or at university. Some students find that the demands we make of them to reason clearly and to support their conclusions rigorously are intellectually exciting. This, at least, is my experience in introducing students to philosophy. Almost all students find those demands harder to satisfy than the demands made of them at previous stages of their education. Their subjection to new norms of argument and the felt difficulty of satisfying them are salient parts of their education. Scheffler's reasoning suggests that by subjecting students to those norms and modeling allegiance to them ourselves, we can foster an academic friendship in which students admire allegiance to those norms and aspire to become the kind of persons who act from them.

Perhaps we can. And perhaps if we succeed, our students will hold their beliefs about how to live less dogmatically and complacently. But if we try to encourage allegiance to abstract norms of reasoning and argument, we risk combating dogmatism by encouraging another trait that we lament in our students: the familiar propensity to aim, debaterlike, at victory in argument rather than at truth. In philosophy, we also run a risk Kyla Ebels-Duggan refers to in her contribution to this volume. Philosophy can muster strong arguments for and against so many ethical positions that students may come to think their own desires are the only bases for deciding how to live. In that case, what is supposed to be an education for autonomy will prove self-undermining, since students will not end up guiding their lives by the authority of their own *reason* after all.

I am, however, skeptical that we could succeed in the way that I have taken Scheffler's article to suggest. One reason for my skepticism is that the line of thought seems to me to rest upon a false premise. In my experience, what is salient for college students, even beginners, is not their subjection to unfamiliar and rigorous standards of reasoning that are applied impersonally across disciplines. It is, rather, that they are subject to demanding norms by this or that professor, and to norms that are specific to philosophy or to English composition or to textual interpretation or—for my most advanced students—to real analysis. This suggests that as we try to model qualities of autonomy, we have to bear in mind that those qualities are exercised while we reason in ways, and take up questions, that are discipline specific. Thinking about how we might do so brings to light other qualities of mind that we would like to encourage in our students besides those I have identified thus far as contributing to autonomy. To see what those qualities are, I want to return to the question of why education for autonomy is thought to be so important.

III

In the previous section, I conjectured that the reason autonomy is so often taken as a goal of formal education, including higher education, is that educators perceive or assume a widespread dogmatism or unthinking deference in their students that they wish to combat. I tried to suggest how an education for autonomy might remedy these shortcomings without contesting the diagnosis.

Although I teach at a Catholic university at which almost all of the students self-identify as religious and have had considerable religious education, I do not find my undergraduates to be particularly dogmatic. Nor do I find them to be uncharitable readers, if by that is meant that they are anxious to score points against a text by counterarguments that are often facile.[16] Rather, the shortcoming I find to be much more common can be illustrated by recounting an experience I often have when I introduce students to great texts in the history of ethics. That is, they read the authors as thinking about the moral life in roughly the way that the students themselves do. Thus many of them read Plato, Aristotle, Aquinas, and Kant all as valuing authenticity, nonjudgmentalism, service, and well-roundedness. Sustaining these interpretations requires students to go to great lengths to locate their own views in the texts and demands considerable hermeneutic ingenuity. More important for present purposes, it also reflects a blinkered imagination.

This constriction of the imagination is not to be confused with the dogmatism that education for autonomy is supposed to remedy. The dogmatist is able to entertain the possibility that the author under consideration defends very different conclusions than he or she does but insists that the author is wrong to do so. Because the students I have in mind read into texts views that they take to be not just true but obviously so, it never crosses their minds that the fundamental questions of human life have been posed and answered in many different ways. This poverty of the imagination does not just limit the ways students read texts. It also limits their ability to imagine and pursue intellectual and moral options that are open to them. It therefore restricts their freedom, albeit in a very different way than dogmatism would. Dogmatism restricts freedom by undermining self-direction; poverty of the imagination restricts it by reducing what students regard as live possibilities. It follows that an education that enriches students' imaginations promises to enhance their freedom in a very different way than education for autonomy as I have discussed it so far.[17]

Once this kind of enhancement is taken to be a goal of higher education, we need to revisit the question of what contributions we who serve on college and university faculties can make to its attainment. I suggested at the end of the previous section that the qualities we most obviously model for our students are discipline specific or are exercised across disciplines but modeled by us, their teachers, in discipline-specific ways. So to address the question of what contributions we can make to the attainment of the goal, it will help to ask what contributions college and university professors are well suited to make by virtue of our disciplinary training.

That training is advanced and quite often doctoral level. To complete it, we had to spend years mastering what had already been achieved in our disciplines. One of the reasons we were drawn to work of that kind, I think, is that we are inspired—rather than repelled or defeated—by the depth and complexity of what has already been achieved in our areas of study. The achievement that drew us into and that holds us to our academic disciplines may be the contrapuntal structure of a Bach fugue, the lovely architectonic of John Rawls's theory of justice, the beautiful proofs of equilibrium results in economics, the ways Cicero and Augustine exploited the syntactic possibilities of classical Latin, the elegant equations of quantum electrodynamics, or a thousand other things. But whatever those achievements are, we who have done advanced disciplinary work are unusual in being excited by them.

In some classes, at least, we have the opportunity to teach our students about the material whose complexity excites us. Their coming to understand the complexity of that material by working through it—laying out arguments, analyzing fugal or syntactic structure, or solving problems—is an exercise of students' reason. The exercise can be arduous, but the processes of gradual discovery and deepening appreciation can also be sources of great pleasure. One reason they can be sources of pleasure is that coming to understand a new style of painting or of music, of writing or of proof, often requires the application of new concepts by which to analyze and describe our experiences. Appreciating the best exemplars of those styles is a matter of learning to see in those paintings, musical compositions, novels, or proofs complexities that would have eluded, confused, or bored us without the right education. Learning thus enriches experience, and the enrichment of experience holds the promise of new intellectual pleasures. Those of us who love learning enjoy such pleasures. We can communicate our enthusiasm for them to our students in hopes that they will become the kind of persons who enjoy those pleasures as well.

Analysis of a text, of a musical piece, of use of language, of a scientific or social scientific theory also brings to light the accomplishment involved in the work analyzed. Those of us who teach these works are well positioned to appreciate those accomplishments because, having worked through them ourselves and tried to make specialized contributions of our own, we understand just how hard-won they were. And so two more things that we can communicate to our students that they may not get from anyone else are an enthusiasm for the great accomplishments of the human mind as such and a heightened appreciation of what tremendous accomplishments they are.

Coming to understand those accomplishments can bring students considerable satisfaction. We college teachers have all seen students grow in confidence and self-respect as they gain some command of difficult material. It can also, and should, induce humility. To come to understand intellectual accomplishment is to come to see how hard intellectual problems are, how resistant they are to human understanding, and how talented and hardworking are the people who have offered answers to them that are worth studying.

Moreover, I take the creation of beauty, the pursuit of knowledge of the natural and social worlds, and the attempt to understand the human condition to be pursuits whose importance is obvious. And I take a nuanced and informed appreciation of what has been achieved in these pursuits—of artistic and intellectual achievements—to be part of a well-lived life. One of the reasons is that the importance of the pursuits in which these achievements are won may not be obvious to students. Seeing the standards by which success in them is reckoned, and gaining some appreciation of how works have been fashioned that meet those standards, should lead students to value those pursuits because they are activities to which intrinsic goods of beauty, knowledge, and understanding are internal. Another reason I take appreciation of great achievements of the human mind to be important is that they are great achievements of the *human* mind. They are the achievements of members of our species who are engaged in practices created and sustained by us. Appreciating them should move students to respect the faculties of which all human beings have a share and thereby, it is hoped, to respect for humanity itself. I therefore take encouraging such appreciation to be among the goals of a humanistic education and hence among the goals at which every college education—whether at a religious or nonreligious institution—should aim.

But I assume that even if we who have done advanced disciplinary work love intellectual intricacy, we do not love it just for its own sake or just because appreciating it advances humanistic values. I assume we are also drawn to it because we think it suits the intricacy and complexity of the world.[18] What this means may be clearest in the physical or social sciences, which make use of mathematical models to describe the objects of inquiry. But I assume the same is true in the arts and humanities, where complicated interpretations may be needed to bring out the nuances of the work under consideration, and where works themselves must be nuanced to do justice to the human realities they explore.

The intellectual complexity that interests me most in the present connection is that to which I am most attracted and with which I am best acquainted: the complexity of philosophy. The best practitioners of that discipline have always assumed that progress can be made only by uncompromising rigor, insistence on the significance of fine distinctions, and careful examination of the questions being posed and the answers being floated. Deep understanding of philosophical texts draws on the same skills to recover the problems with which those texts are concerned, the answers they propound, and the alternative questions and answers they reject or overlook. The historical, exegetical, and systematic questions with which philosophers are concerned demand that these skills be brought to bear. It is their exercise that gives philosophical work its distinctive kinds of complexity and exactness.

The need to draw distinctions, multiply questions, and clarify concepts is as pressing in practical philosophy as it is in other areas of the discipline because moral reality itself is complicated. The conference at which the contributions to this volume were first presented was subtitled "Problems of Morality and Justice." Those who study these problems and their history are aware of how wide a range of considerations bear upon them. It is hard to know whether some of those considerations trump others absolutely or whether they should be balanced, and if so, how. We know how hard it is to pose problems of morality and justice in tractable form, and we know that philosophers have identified very different problems as central. Moreover, we have all had the experience of thinking that we know enough to make some progress on a problem, only to read something that shows us dimensions of that problem of which we had previously been unaware, dimensions that have been painstakingly explored by others whose work we find we need to learn. Thus intellectual work in moral and political philosophy—as in other areas of philosophy and, I assume, as in all areas of inquiry, humanistic, mathematical, and scientific—is regularly punctuated by reminders of a familiar truth: the problems on which we are working are harder than we thought.

Speaking for myself, I find the first glimpse of new intellectual territory to be a bracing experience. While the thought of entering virgin space is intimidating, I look forward to exploring new territory when I know that I can make my way through it with the help of scholars who have gone before me. The prospect of eventually being able to look at a fascinating problem from a different place is part of what keeps me going. In this, I assume I am like most college and university professors who are sustained in our work by the joy of discovery. The real benefit of realizing how hard our problems are is not, however, the pleasure that accompanies progress and insight. It is the brake that that realization provides. Seeing how hard intellectual problems are—including moral and political problems—and seeing how much can and should be learned about them greatly diminishes the attraction of simple answers and of those that are most commonly accepted. Appreciation of complexity halts the precipitate march to premature conclusions.

Our students are not naturally sensitive to the difficulty of moral and political problems. My own experience is that even before they can entertain answers, they have to learn to be bothered by the questions and to be shown their many dimensions. And so another thing that we can and should do for our students is show them that even the most familiar human phenomena admit of complex explanations, that they do so because moral and political reality are hard, that the great questions of humanity—and the great questions facing our society—are therefore complicated, and that the easy answers are more likely to merit suspicion than acceptance.

This in itself may alleviate many of the intellectual shortcomings college and university faculty say they detect in their students. Consider again the students I mentioned at the beginning of this section who read their own moral views into great texts in the history of philosophical and religious ethics. I opined that the reason they do so is not that they hold their views dogmatically, but that they are unable to imagine alternatives. They do not know enough about moral thinking to imagine that someone might look at the moral world very differently from the way they do, with different conceptions of human happiness and fulfillment or wrongdoing and guilt. And so the other, less strained and more faithful interpretations that classic works might bear simply do not occur to them.

Part of teaching students about the complexity of the moral world is recovering the questions posed by great thinkers of the past and showing why those thinkers posed the questions they did. Another part is assessing the answers to those questions, both according to the standards used by the thinkers who offered them and by standards of adequacy for us. Because of the difficulty of moral and political problems, I do not think we can offer knockdown arguments for, or marshal the full authority of reason behind, answers to those problems. We who explore these problems in our teaching can indicate what arguments we find most compelling and present them forcefully while openly acknowledging the difficulties with them. What we *must* do is show students that their initial formulations of questions and answers need considerable refinement.

Showing them even that much is freeing, and in a different way from the education for autonomy discussed in the previous section. For as students come to understand how differently the human world has been conceived at different times and by different thinkers, the various ways in which they might live, including the various ways they might understand and live their religious tradition, are greatly multiplied. Removing the blinkers from their moral and religious imaginations by multiplying possibilities frees them from the self-imposed necessity of choosing from a small number of familiar options.

Of course, even if students' imaginations become less constricted as a result of education, they still need the confidence to explore newly opened possibilities. That confidence may not be easily found. My tentative generalization about students is that many of the traits that we think we see in them—uncritical acceptance of answers provided by a moral or religious authority, a tradition or a revered text; facile debating; the toleration of any intellectual or moral position whatever; the tendency to read all authors as agreeing with them—stem at least in part from a desire for simple solutions to the problems of life. This desire, in turn, stems in part from an understandable aversion to intellectual effort and in part from the conflation of simplistic clarity with toughness and moral strength. But I think students, like many other people, also seek simple solutions because they find comfort in the thought that the world, including the moral world, is easily comprehended. The recognition that it is not is part of intellectual maturity. It is also a quality of mind that is needed to live a good life and to be a good citizen. Encouraging it should be one of the goals of a college or university education. In the next section, I shall suggest a way college and university faculty can do so.

IV

In section II, I argued that if we are to educate students for autonomy as that is usually understood, we must encourage them to become the kind of people whom their reason moves by the exercise of its authority. In section III, I argued that there are other exercises of their reason that we also want to affect them. We want our students to admire the complexity of great intellectual accomplishments and to appreciate what makes those accomplishments great. We want them to take pride in gaining some understanding of those achievements but also to be humbled by their magnitude. We want them to respect human reason and humanity itself. We want them to be moved in the right way by the complexity of the world, including the human world, so that they do not shy away from the difficulty of moral and political problems or seek refuge in easy solutions.

If students are to become persons who are affected in these ways, their education must do more than develop their intelligence. It must also shape their cares, their tastes, and their desires. For example, if they are to appreciate great works of literature or philosophy, economics or music or physics, they have to develop a taste for intellectual beauty and elegance. If they are to take pride in the mastery of difficult material, they have to care about learning and regard it as a worthy accomplishment. If they are not to shy away from unfamiliar and difficult answers to the questions of life, they need to develop intellectual courage and steadfastness in the pursuit of truth. How are these qualities of mind to be encouraged?

As with the desire to follow the authority of reason, so with the desires associated with the qualities of mind discussed in section III, it is not altogether clear what the desires are desires for. But I assume that they include or are enhanced by the desire to be a certain kind of person. If that is right, then we who teach should try to cultivate that desire by being the kind of person we think students should want to be. We can do that by modeling the qualities of mind we want them to acquire. And so as we teach our discipline to our students, we can model enthusiasm for its intricacy, depth, and beauty.

Of course, whether our modeling these enthusiasms inspires them in our students depends upon whether they will want their education to make them the kind of persons our professional training has made us. That they will may seem unlikely. The fact that few of our undergraduates follow us into the academy suggests that few of them develop the desire to emulate us. That failure may be overdetermined, but one explanation would surely appeal to the powerful peer and pecuniary pressures that incline students to value their learning instrumentally rather than intrinsically. It would be unrealistic to believe that we can successfully countervail those pressures in very many cases or that we can inspire powerful intellectual enthusiasms that persist through the whole of our students' lives. What we can realistically hope to do, I think, is inspire enthusiasms and aspirations that fire them for a time and that have enduring effects. I suggest that we can do so by forming academic friendships with our students, so that they come to see those qualities of mind that they want to develop at least for the duration of their time with their professor. How can such a friendship be built?

In the first section, I likened academic friendships to friendships among fellow travelers, one of whom guides the others. We can start building such friendships with our students from the time we start to guide them, by starting with some phenomenon that they think they understand—a familiar political phenomenon like voting or a familiar moral one like the attempt to live a good life—and show them how deeply puzzling it is. Through the course of our time with them, we can make evident how much we love the intellectual puzzles and the solutions that have been offered to them. And we can communicate how much we want our students to love them too. By working with them, evincing concern with their progress, and allying with them against the difficulty of material that we, too, want to understand more deeply, we can guide them to the shared goods of intellectual discovery. The sharing of these goods among those who share a classroom can engender a sense of community. In my experience, that sense of community is often enhanced by students' acquisition of a new, shared idiom that is drawn from the philosophical material we are working on and that becomes a transient part of their working vocabulary. I suggest that when students feel they are part of a classroom community led by a professor who evidently cares about sharing broadening educational experiences with them, they respond by developing—at least in nascent form—the qualities of mind that we model for them and want them to acquire.

The academic friendships I have described grow out of the shared good of progressing in a particular area of intellectual inquiry. At the end of section II, I drew on Samuel Scheffler's work to raise the possibility that academic friendship might "derive . . . from the shared experience of subjection . . . to normativity itself." This normativity is that expressed by the norms of evidence and reasoning to which we hold our students. I do not deny that solidarity might develop among students, and between students and their professors, as a result of their attempt to comply with those norms. But if it does, it will be because students have learned to care about complying with them, because they have come to see it as something they want to do. I doubt that students will care about complying with those norms apart from wanting to think well about the subject matter of one or another academic discipline. If this doubt is well founded, then—if students do come to care about such compliance for its own sake—what they will care about for *its* own sake is reasoning well about the subject matter of a particular discipline. And if that is right, then the kind of academic friendship I drew on Scheffler's essay to identify presupposes that professors have successfully inspired the care for their subjects that I have said we should model.

One of the ways in which the academic friendship of professors and students is like that among fellow travelers is that both kinds of friendship are generally of limited duration. However successfully we create communities of learning in our classrooms, those communities disband at the end of the quarter or the semester or the academic year. This raises the possibility that the desires and cares we try to encourage in our students will cease to motivate them, at best to be replaced by those encouraged in other classes. But even if that is so, we should not conclude that these qualities of mind will vanish when our work with students ceases. The experiences of a journey can have a lasting impact even after the vividness of our travel experiences fades. Indeed, one of the ways that the most vivid experiences of travel can broaden and educate us is by shaping our tastes, thereby disposing us to respond to later experiences differently than we otherwise would have.

This effect of travel was given eloquent expression by Henry James, who, at the end of roughly a semester's visit to Rome, wrote:

> One would like to be able after five months in Rome to sum up for tribute and homage, one's experience, one's gains, the whole adventure of one's sensibility. But one really has vibrated too much—the addition of so many items isn't easy. What is simply clear is the sense of an acquired passion for the place and of an incalculable number of gathered impressions. Many of these have been intense and momentous, but one has trodden on the other—there are always the big fish that swallow up the little—and one can hardly say what has become of them. They store themselves noiselessly away, I suppose, in the dim but safe places of memory and "taste," and we live in a quiet faith that they will emerge into vivid relief if life or art should demand them.[19]

We can hope that the qualities of mind we try to model for our students can remain as dispositions that will be triggered when "life . . . should demand them" by confronting students with questions that they have studied with us.

V

It may be objected that the conception of academic friendship I have sketched is highly idealized, since it makes very optimistic assumptions about student responsiveness to our teaching, and it presupposes the kind of teaching that only those who work at elite institutions are able to offer. The kind of partnership in learning that I have described seems most likely to develop in small classes in which professors can get to know their students, learn what interests them, and track their progress closely. It may well be that few colleges and universities can afford to make such classes available to their teachers and students. Even if many do now, it is almost certain that fewer will be able or willing to do so in the future.[20] And if that is right, then the education I have described, like the travel to which I have likened it, is a privilege that either is not now widely available or one that increasing financial pressure will make less common.

I offer just three too-brief replies.

First, if the conception I have sketched is indeed idealized, then it must be something of an educational ideal. Ideal theory is as useful in the philosophy of education as elsewhere. One of its uses is to help us see more clearly where and why teaching and learning that depart from it fall short. The availability of small classes is often used as a measure of the quality of education a college or university offers. The discussion of academic friendship may help to show why such classes are desirable and what students are losing when the only classes available to them are impersonal because they are large. Another way in which the discussion may prove useful is in critiquing the aims of professors at institutions that *are* able to offer small classes. Small classes can also be impersonal if faculty fail to develop an academic friendship with their students because they view a lighter grading load primarily as an opportunity to do their own research. Someone who treats small classes in that way incurs an opportunity cost himself and imposes an opportunity cost on his students. Greater appreciation of the value of academic friendship can help us to see just how high that cost is and what a dereliction of our duty it is to impose it.

Secondly, at least our best students enjoy a wide range of opportunities upon graduation. Some of those opportunities will be lucrative, in the long run if not the short. Sometimes parental pressures, peer pressures, the pressures of educational debt, the unspoken equation of success with wealth, and the desire to enjoy at least an upper middle-class life can incline the best graduates of the best universities to pursue opportunities that promise financial rewards. Their unthinking choice to do so is often lamented, and rightly so.[21] If our students are to be dissuaded from such a choice, the dissuasion is likely to come from people who know them, whom they admire, and who have their interests at heart. If we teachers have developed academic friendships with them and have modeled a commitment to intellectual life, we will be much better positioned to join with others in persuading them that ways of life dedicated to the pursuit of other values are at least as choice-worthy as the careers so many of them now decide to pursue.

Finally, I have said that one of the ends of academic friendship is to remove the blinkers from students' imaginations. The actual is a particularly powerful constraint on the imagination. In particular, the pervasiveness and familiarity of injustice in our world incline us to think that such injustice is natural, and the illusion of its naturalness makes it hard for us to imagine how else the world might be. To adapt a thought of John Rawls's, injustice can seem as natural a feature of our world as our own mortality,[22] and it can be as hard to imagine a world without the former as one without the latter. The broadening of students' moral and political imaginations, at a time of life when many of them are inclined to idealism anyway, can break the hold of the actual and help students to think, carefully and rigorously, about how different the social world might be. Our students will go on to be citizens, participants and perhaps leaders in the worlds of work, civil society, and politics. We therefore have a responsibility to help broaden their imaginations.

Bibliography

Aristotle. Nicomachean Ethics. In The Basic Works of Aristotle, edited by Richard McKeon. New York: Random House, 1941.

Arneson, Richard, and Ian Shapiro. "Democratic Autonomy and Religious Freedom: A Critique of Wisconsin v. Yoder." In Democracy's Place, edited by Ian Shapiro. Ithaca, NY: Cornell University Press, 1996. 137–74.

Aumann, Robert. "Autobiography," http://www.nobelprize.org/nobel_prizes/economics /laureates/2005/aumann-autobio.html. Accessed April 9, 2012.

Brighouse, Harry. "Civic Education and Liberal Legitimacy," Ethics 108 (1998): 719–45.

Dietrich, Franz and Christian List. "Where Do Preferences Come From?," http://personal .lse.ac.uk/list/PDF-files/DietrichListPreferences.pdf. Accessed May 14, 2013.

Gutmann, Amy. "Civic Education and Social Diversity." Ethics 105 (1995): 557–79.

———. Democratic Education. Princeton, NJ: Princeton University Press, 1999.

Hart, Sergiu. "An Interview with Robert Aumann." Macroeconomic Dynamics 9 (2005): 683–740.

James, Henry. Italian Hours. New York: Penguin, 1995.

Klein, Ezra. "Harvard's Liberal Arts Failure is Wall Street's Gain," http://mobile.bloomberg .com/news/2012-02-16/harvard-liberal-arts-failure-is-wall-street-gain-commentary -by-ezra-klein. Accessed April 15, 2012.

Oliff, Phil, Vincent Palacios, Ingrid Johnson, and Michael Leachman. "Recent Deep State Higher Education Cuts May Harm Students and the Economy for Years to Come,", Center on Budget and Policy Priorities white paper, http://www.cbpp.org/cms/?fa =view&id=3927. Accessed May 14, 2013.

Özerdem, Alpl. "The Commodification of Higher Education: The Pedagogical Costs?" Forum: Enhancing Teaching and Learning at the University of York 16 (2007): 1–2.

Rawls, John. A Theory of Justice. Cambridge, MA: Harvard University Press, 1999.

Scheffler, Samuel. "The Good of Toleration." In Equality and Tradition: Questions of Value in Moral and Political Theory, edited by Samuel Scheffler. New York: Oxford University Press, 2010. 312–35.

Weithman, Paul, "Deliberative Character." Journal of Political Philosophy 13 (2005): 263–83.

———. "Education for Political Autonomy." In Wisdom of the Christian Faith, edited by Paul Moser and Michael McFall. Cambridge: Cambridge University Press, 2012.

Notes

I am grateful to my colleagues Fred Freddoso and Gary Gutting, whose insights into university teaching have greatly contributed to the way I think of it. I am also grateful to Harry Brighouse and to anonymous reviewers of this volume for their helpful suggestions on this essay.

1. Aristotle (1941), VIII, 3.
2. Ibid., VIII, 4, at 1157a14.
3. See Özerdem (2007), 1–2.
4. Since rational choice theory takes preferences to be exogenously given; see Franz Dietrich and Christian List, "Where Do Preferences Come From?," http://personal .lse.ac.uk/list/PDF-files/DietrichListPreferences.pdf (accessed May 14, 2013).
5. Aristotle (1941), VIII, 9, at 1159b27ff.
6. Ibid., VIII, 5.
7. Ibid., IX, 9.
8. Ibid., VIII, 6.
9. Arneson and Shapiro (1996), 167–71.
10. I explore some aspects of the distinction between political and perfectionist arguments in Weithman (2012).
11. Gutmann (1999), 77.
12. Brighouse (1998), 728.
13. When is someone prepared to engage in public deliberation? The answer has to be: once he or she has a family of intellectual and deliberative dispositions. That is, one is prepared only if one has the right attitude toward one's own views, and one has the right attitude toward one's own views only if it is true of a person that he or she would respond in the proper ways if presented with arguments of certain kinds. And so saying with any precision just what attitudes educators should encourage requires spelling out counterfactuals that quickly become very complicated. I have tried to do that in Weithman (2005).
14. See, e.g., Gutmann (1995), 572.
15. Scheffler (2010), 332.
16. However, in her contribution to this volume Kyla Ebels-Duggan indicates that she does find that shortcoming in her students.
17. Since I think expanding students' imagination in the way that I have suggested enhances their ability to deliberate about their own conceptions of the good, I take this line of thought to support one of the defenses of the humanities offered by Christopher Bertram in his contribution to this volume.
18. There are, of course, exceptions. See Hart (2005), 686–87. Aumann makes the same point in his "Autobiography," http://www.nobelprize.org/nobel_prizes/economics /laureates/2005/aumann-autobio.html (accessed April 9, 2012).
19. James (1995), 193.
20. See Oliff, Palacios, Johnson, and Leachman, "Recent Deep State Higher Education

Cuts May Harm Students and the Economy for Years to Come," white paper, http://www.cbpp.org/cms/?fa=view&id=3927 (accessed May 14, 2013).

21. See, e.g., Klein, "Harvard's Liberal Arts Failure Is Wall Street's Gain," http://mobile.bloomberg.com/news/2012-02-16/harvard-liberal-arts-failure-is-wall-street-gain-commentary-by-ezra-klein (accessed April 15, 2012).

22. Rawls (1999), 91.

FIVE

Autonomy as Intellectual Virtue

KYLA EBELS-DUGGAN

Promoting students' autonomy is widely affirmed as an important aim of education generally and higher education in particular. Ultimately, I will join in this affirmation, but only after situating the development of autonomy in the context of a broader aim and interpreting it in a revisionary way. The broader aim is the development of students' intellectual virtues, and my interpretation of autonomy conceives it in perhaps surprising terms. In particular, I'll argue that the truth in the autonomy view is captured by the thesis that education should aim to foster the intellectual virtues of *charity* and *humility*.

I begin by laying out what I take to be a standard conception of the autonomy view. The position has three parts: (1) a diagnosis of the typical problem or threat to students' autonomy, which is a characterization of heteronomy; (2) a prescription or practical recommendation for how to address the threat; and (3) a prognosis, a conception of the autonomy that the prescription aims to produce.

I oppose all three elements of this standard conception. First, I'll question its diagnosis of the most significant obstacles to intellectual maturity that the typical student faces and suggest an alternative. This will lead in to concerns about the appropriateness of the recommended treatment. I'll suggest that the standard prescription may tend to exacerbate rather than ameliorate common intellectual vices. I'll then lay out an alternative prognosis, or goal at which I think that education should aim. This goal includes a reconceptualization of autonomy as humility and charity, embedded in the larger aim of facilitating intellectual virtues. I'll suggest that, despite my disagreements with the standard approach, my position succeeds in capturing what is right about it: students who develop humility and charity do not lack any further characteristic helpfully called "autonomy." At the end of the chapter I'll go further, though in a more tentative spirit, raising doubts about whether autonomy so conceived is desirable with respect to all commitments. In fact, there may be no way to characterize a relationship in which we ought to stand to our intellectual commitments that is independent of their content.[1]

I. The Standard View

The standard view is so standard that it's difficult to find formal scholarly statements, but informal endorsements are myriad.[2] Here is just one example, a philosophy professor giving her view about her role as an educator on the occasion of receiving a prestigious teaching award: she says that "her job is to challenge the assumptions and beliefs that students have when they arrived at [the university]." And she adds, "They may leave . . . endorsing the same beliefs they came here with, but if they do so reflectively and for reasons they can articulate, then I've done my job."[3] Not long ago I would have wholeheartedly endorsed this worthy-sounding goal. In what follows I attempt to articulate my rising doubts.

Begin with the standard diagnosis. In this story, students typically enter college standing in some problematic relation to a particular set of ideas, a tradition of thought, or a conception of the good. The standard view often treats the commitments of the family of origin as the primary threat. Growing up in a family committed to a certain value outlook is regarded as a risk factor for taking on value commitments heteronomously, and formal education as a counterweight that works against this risk.[4] Traditional religious views are often treated as paradigmatic,[5] but occasionally autonomy advocates include among their stated targets commitment to purely intellectual traditions. Martha Nussbaum worries about students treating books, especially those identified as "great books," as authorities: "Often, however, so great is [books'] prestige that they actually lull pupils into forgetfulness of the activity of mind that is education's real goal, teaching them to be passively reliant on the written word. Such pupils, having internalized a lot of culturally authoritative material, may come to believe that they are very wise . . . books are all too likely to become objects of veneration and deference" (Nussbaum, *Cultivating Humanity*, 34–35). Despite these paradigm examples, the most common version of the standard view has it that the particular content of students' commitments, whatever it may be, is not at issue. Advocates are often careful to say—as the professor quoted above does—that a student might end his or her education with the same commitments with which he or she began, while nevertheless moving from heteronomy to autonomy. It is thought to be sufficient that students end up holding their views "reflectively and for reasons that they can articulate." The problem, then, is conceived not as the content of students' beliefs but rather as the likelihood of being in the bad relationship with them, holding them heteronomously. On the official story, it's as objectionable to stand in this relationship with respect to true, admirable, or benign value convictions as with respect to false, bad, or dangerous ones.

I find that it is surprisingly difficult to characterize the details of the problematic relation while maintaining the neutrality about content. But let's provisionally adopt some of the language proponents use in describing the view. Sometimes authors speak of the problem in terms of a conception's seeming "inevitable" or "natural."[6] We can try describing the worrisome relationship as being "unreflectively" or "inflexibly" attached to a particular view. This at least lies in the direction of most autonomy advocates' concerns.

It is equally challenging to state clearly the purported right relationship to our views, the conception of autonomy. Even thinkers who give the ideal of autonomy a central place do not always fully articulate their understanding of this relation.[7] But we know that it's supposed to serve as an antidote to heteronomy. So the autonomous person is not unreflectively committed to any one view; no single conception of the good seems inevitable or natural to him or her. Advocates of the standard view often put this in terms of having access to a range of alternatives or feasible options for what to value and how to conceive of a good life.[8]

This then provides the basis for the standard prescription: education for autonomy must give students options by presenting a range of views about what is of value or information about "alternative ways of life." Discussions of this approach in primary and secondary education usually emphasize composing classrooms of students from a variety of cultural and religious traditions, so that they may learn from one another about different points of view.[9] Many writers on higher education are also impressed by the value of having diverse views represented in the classroom, but an adversarial tone foreign to discussions of earlier education sometimes takes hold here. We saw this earlier in the professor's claim that her job is to "challenge assumptions." Nussbaum puts the program of higher education in terms of "confronting" students with alternatives to the views that they accept.[10]

What are students supposed to do with these various conceptions of the good? There is near unanimity that we should teach and encourage them to "think critically" about all of them. After drawing attention to this widespread agreement, Derek Bok helpfully speculates that we attain concord on this point only by leaving the central term vague.[11] This seems absolutely right to me, so unsurprisingly I think that there is something correct, but also something misleading, in discussions of critical thinking. I return to this later.

So the standard view has a diagnosis of a central problem that education aims to address, a prescription for how to counter this problem, and a prognosis for what the recommended program of education will produce. The diagnosis is that students tend to be wrongly attached to a particular conception of the good, often the traditional views of their family of origin. The prescription is critical engagement with a wide variety of conceptions of the good. The prognosis is that students will become able to choose freely from among these conceptions the one that suits them best. Thus educated students are liberated from the heteronomous inheritance of a single conception and given instead a range of options from which they may make their own autonomous choice.

II. Questioning the Diagnosis

I find that this standard picture of college students tenaciously attached to a traditional conception of the good has very limited application to my experience. For instance, I encounter relatively few students with the well-defined religious commitments often supposed to typify the problem, and those who have them seem well aware of live alternatives. As far as I can tell, almost none experience such commitments as altogether natural or inevitable, holding them—in this sense—unreflectively. On the whole they strike me as rather more likely than others to have reflected on their outlook, bringing it into view as an object of consideration and considering seriously the possibility that it may be wrong. If there is a problem with the way that most religious students hold their views, we need some other terms in which to characterize it.

The news that unwavering commitment to an intellectual tradition is rarer still will surprise no one. I confess to some envy of the problems that Nussbaum reports. Never have I encountered a student who has been rendered passive by the internalization of a lot of culturally relevant material and has a tendency to venerate books. In fact I would begin a characterization of intellectual vices with which I am more familiar by citing the opposite problem: if I give my students Plato or Aristotle, Aquinas or Kant, those who treat it as worth engaging at all often act as if they can tell me immediately why it is wrong. I find that the hard work of teaching often takes the shape of convincing or inspiring students to take these—or any—texts seriously as something from which they might learn something positive, something that might actually matter, not just for their grade for the class, but for their lives outside of the classroom.

So one intellectual vice that I do commonly see in students is a certain overconfidence in critical stance, especially toward texts. Such overconfidence could be driven by unduly stubborn commitment to, and defensiveness of, some traditional view, and once in a while it is. But much, much more often it is paired with a professed lack of positive convictions about normative matters. I offer, by way of illustration, two examples from a recent freshman seminar. First, no student among the fifteen in my class would admit sympathy with the view that Rawls's grass counter is wasting his time. Even worse, none would defend, and most denied, the view that if society evolved to a point at which most people regarded killing another person as of no more consequence than killing a bug, this would count as a moral decline.

I resist concluding that students genuinely hold these normative positions. Surely one thing that is going on in such moments is that they are acting strategically, doing their best to adapt to the sometimes unfamiliar norms of the classroom. It is not hard to believe that students experience themselves as unable to defend their actual commitments in what probably appears to them the foreign language and style of a college seminar. In response, they adopt a pragmatic attitude, limiting their professed commitments in a way calculated to avoid exposure as inarticulate in front of their peers and to secure a good grade in the class.

But to the extent that this accurately describes what is happening, it reveals serious problems with the way that we are structuring the incentives of the classroom. These incentives are predictable, if unintended, effects of the standard prescription, a point that I take up in section III. It would be bad enough if the results were contained in the classroom, but we have reason to think that habits of forgoing or disowning positive value commitments characterize our students' ethical thought more generally. A sociological study conducted in 2008 found widespread evidence of the phenomenon among young adults.[12] The authors of the study characterize their findings this way: "What we have found, in short, is that moral individualism is widespread among emerging adults and that a sizable minority professes to believe in moral relativism."[13] The authors use "moral individualism" to refer to the view that "morality is a personal choice, entirely a matter of individual decision. Moral rights and wrongs are essentially matters of individual opinion. . . . 'It's personal,' [the respondents] typically say. 'It's up to the individual. Who am I to say?'"[14] To my mind, this unwillingness to stake out and stand for substantive value commitments is the largest obstacle to the intellectual maturity of many of today's students.

Taken to its limit, this practiced lack of conviction yields a positive view about value, despite its practitioners' intentions. It's a commonplace in philosophy departments that students arrive affirming a crude subjectivism, which has thus earned the name "freshman relativism." Another of the interviewees in the study just mentioned gives us a version of the view: "I mean, I guess what makes something right is how I feel about it. But different people feel different ways, so I couldn't speak on behalf of anyone else as to what's right and wrong."[15] The freshman relativist thinks that something is valuable or good or right for a person just if that person wants, desires, or likes it. Or something like that; it is the exceptional student who has gotten so far as to formulate the position. Nevertheless, if there's a view that incoming college students typically hold unreflectively, this is it.

The subjectivist view stands in an interesting and troubling relationship to another major influence on students' thinking. Harry Brighouse—in an exception to autonomy advocates' focus on traditionalist views—identifies as the primary threat to autonomy "a public and particularly a popular culture that is governed by commercial forces that dedicate considerable resources to undermining children's prospective autonomy, aiming to inculcate a life-long and unreflective materialism."[16] It should not go unnoted that the subjectivist position about value fits nicely with the aims of the commercial forces with which Brighouse is concerned. The idea that wanting something makes it good provides scant leverage for a critique of materialism.[17] In fact, to the extent that these forces aim to promote some general view about value, it seems to be just such a desire-based subjectivism.

So, in my experience, students tend toward overconfidence in, or at least overstatement of, their critiques and rejections of possible positions coupled with a lack of conviction about their positive views. It is at best a small minority of students whose weakness is too much deference to the perceived moral authority of some tradition, and we're likely to fail to meet students' needs if we conceive this as their paradigmatic problem.

III. Questioning the Prescription

An incorrect diagnosis generates an unhelpful prescription. Indeed, as I've just suggested, the intellectual vices that concern me are plausibly, in part, effects of the standard prescription. In the education that many autonomy advocates imagine, a student is presented with a range of views about some normative matter, with the aim of putting him or her in a position to choose among them. But it is difficult to present different views fairly without suggesting the metaview that all are equally worthy of choice. And then it can seem that one's own preferences or desires are the only possible basis for decision among them. Most of today's college students have earlier educational experiences that fit this model. Their internalization of the subjectivism it suggests would be an unsurprising result, even though this is almost never what autonomy advocates intend.[18]

An emphasis on critical thinking, if not carefully managed, can make matters worse. As Bok reminds us, "critical thinking" means many things to many people, but surely one thing to which it refers is the skill of identifying flawed reasoning. In our rhetoric-drenched society, the ability to spot a bad argument is certainly valuable and deserves the widespread endorsement that it enjoys among educators. But in emphasizing this skill we risk communicating a primarily negative vision of the intellectual enterprise. Critical thinking, in the sense of spotting flaws, is something that better-educated students develop in high school, and many readily wield this tool against whatever texts they find on their syllabi. Since it is almost always easier to attack a position than to defend one, intelligent and strategically minded students are especially drawn to this approach. These texts shouldn't be immune from critique, of course, but it is easy to see how such critical abilities could flower into the negative stance that I described earlier.

Focusing on critical thinking also encourages students to play the role of the skeptic demanding arguments at every turn. Faced with even the most innocuous normative claim—for example, *it is wrong to torture someone just for fun*—some students will demand a compelling line of reasoning before giving assent. Though, like most philosophers, I am a big fan of reasons and argument, I think that such challenges can bring with them dangerously hyperrationalist presuppositions. Such demands often suggest that one is entitled to a position only if one can give a complete defense of it, a defense that would—or at least should—convince a skeptic.[19] It is not at all clear that any commitment would be able to meet this standard. Indeed, it is often not clear what would even count as meeting it. To what premises could one appeal that are more secure than the conclusion sought? If the imagined skeptic is willing to reject the claim that it's wrong to torture for fun, what is he or she willing to accept?

Because it is difficult to see what could answer such questions, students can successfully level the critical demand against almost any normative commitment. This makes skepticism an attractive strategy for those who treat classroom discussion as a game to be won. But such challenges can also serve as a shield against considering the real appeal of any particular positive view. Treating ideas in this way tends to divorce the work of the classroom from genuine ethical reflection while alienating those who are amenable to thinking seriously about matters of value. At the same time, these critical habits feed both the overconfident negative stance and the corresponding lack of positive conviction that I mentioned above.

Marching students through a bunch of options and demonstrating the problems with each is standard practice in most college classes that deal with normative issues. But it is far from clear that this is the best way to address the needs of the students I've described. Most come to us aware of the existence of a multitude of purported normative options, and many are good at spotting the problems with them. Such students are often already prone to conclude that questions about value can only be settled by appeal to preference or personal taste. "Confronting" whatever further value convictions some may nevertheless have with a demand for "reasons they can articulate" risks communicating that they should abandon these commitments unless they have an argument that would meet all comers. But this is an impossibly high, and therefore unhelpful, bar. I worry, then, that the standard prescription is producing a generation of students who are good at rejecting ideas but lack the ability to recognize those worth affirming and perhaps even loving. I wonder if, in some cases, students do not even entertain the possibility that any idea could be like this.

IV. A New Prognosis

I've suggested that the standard view wrongly diagnoses the intellectual vices typical of today's students, and that its prescription may tend to exacerbate rather than ameliorate their most common problems. I also think that there are problems with the standard conception of autonomy as one choice among available options for value commitments, a point to which I shall return later. But for all that, I think there is something right about the idea that college instructors should be aiming to facilitate students' autonomy. In this section I try to get at the agreement by suggesting that we reconceive autonomy as an intellectual virtue, or more precisely as a combination of two virtues. I understand virtues in what I take to be a traditional way, as traits of character that counter a particular temptation, weakness, or vice.[20] So I begin here by considering what virtues would serve a student with each of the two vices detailed above: overconfidence in critical stance and lack of positive conviction.

Two closely related virtues serve to counter the vice of overconfidence.

Charity governs encounters with unfamiliar views. The intellectually charitable person approaches new ideas and texts with the presumption that
there is something true and worthwhile to be found there. He or she thus
refrains from immediate criticism, striving first to understand the positions
and to reconstruct them in a way that brings out what seems most plausible.
Humility is a corresponding attitude governing one's relationship to one's
own view. I propose that we understand intellectual humility as, first of all,
a matter of recognizing the genuine difficulty of serious intellectual tasks.
To claim that many important normative questions do not yield to easy
answers is an understatement, and the humble person recognizes this. This
inclines him or her to fallibilism about his or her own views. More importantly, it makes him or her slow to attribute disagreement to intellectual
laziness, stupidity, or moral turpitude on the part of interlocutors.

With these virtues in mind, we can consider anew the student that the
standard conception has in view. Though we never arrived at a fully satisfying characterization of this student, the standard worry that he or she is
unreflective and inflexible in his or her commitments bears a resemblance
to that aspect of my own diagnosis that I call overconfidence. This kinship in
diagnoses suggests that charity and humility might be the right goal for both
sorts of students. So I ask: if the students whom advocates of the standard
view imagine had or developed charity (a willingness to seek truth in unfamiliar views) and humility (a recognition of difficulty and a resulting fallibilism and respect for opponents), would "autonomy" plausibly name some
further trait that they still need? If the answer to this question is negative, as
I think it is, then we have reason to think that these virtues provide a new
and better way of interpreting the goal of autonomy.[21] Thus, even those who
disagree with my diagnosis or face classrooms full of very different students
from my own might well endorse my prognosis, my view about the goals
at which higher education should aim under the heading of "autonomy."

One might think that this conception of autonomy is just what its advocates had in mind all along. But it is prima facie surprising that autonomy,
which right down to its etymology is associated with self-reliance and self-
empowerment, could be identified with charity and humility. I, at any rate,
find thinking in these latter terms a genuinely helpful advance in my understanding of what I am trying to accomplish in my teaching. The reconception allows us to make sense of autonomy as a goal without tempting us to
imagine a standpoint from which a student could freely choose a conception
of the good. That strikes me as good news since, like many others, including most advocates of autonomy, I think that this standpoint is a fantasy.
The reconception also removes the suggestion that having deep normative

convictions is, per se, a problem for or threat to autonomy. And the ideals of charity and humility are not easily confused with subjectivism about value.

The reconception also avoids the standard view's tendency toward conceiving students as on the defensive: we challenge the views they have, and they have to defend them by articulating reasons for them. I think this is how many students experience college-level seminars, especially in the humanities. As I explained earlier, I worry that this approach only feeds the problems. It may be helpful to challenge their critical orientation and/or their lack of confidence in their entitlement to have normative convictions. But these are not so much beliefs or commitments that we can confront. They are, rather, habits of approaching texts and ideas for which we need to model alternatives.

This brings us to the other problem that I identified earlier: lack of conviction. The ideal of charity is relevant here too, insofar as it demands a presumption that others' views have positive insight. One treats a view charitably only if one takes it seriously as a source of truly illuminating ideas, ideas that might help one make sense of one's experience in the world and that one might thus really take on board. Thus an appreciation of positive commitment is built into the ideal and practice of intellectual charity. This also means that taking the development of charity as a goal of education sets us in opposition to students' common tendency to approach academic work in narrowly strategic terms, a tendency that I have suggested the standard view may encourage. So long as a student occupies this instrumental mindset toward the material and class discussion, he or she falls short of charity.

But we should go further than this. Alongside other intellectual virtues, we should aim to foster a virtue that I'll call *tenacity*. Intellectually tenacious people credit the appearance of truth that their own views have and so do not easily abandon them. They are not likely to fall prey to the idea that they are entitled only to those views that they can fully defend against skeptics. Tenacity also opposes the weaker position that they ought to abandon a commitment whenever they lack an answer to an objection to it. If I am right that, on the whole, our students err in the direction of too easy abandonment of substantive normative views, then we should teach and model some willingness to tolerate tension.

V. On Getting It Right

At this point, if not before, some readers will be nervous, perhaps even alarmed. Even those willing to grant that some students could benefit from greater tenacity will likely insist that others could benefit from less. Surely there is tension between charity and humility on the one hand and tenacity on the other, and when students err too much in the direction of the latter, tenacity becomes a vice. I begin this section with an innocuous, but perhaps unhelpful, response at the formal level, one that continues to try to characterize a relationship to their ideas in which we ought to educate students to stand. But I then suggest that we can push this formal approach only so far. In the end, there may be no such commendable relation that is independent of the ideas and commitments that students have. This constitutes a more significant break with the standard autonomy view than I have so far acknowledged and may expose unwelcome complications in articulating the aims of contemporary colleges and universities. Some readers might agree with me up through the formal point but refuse to go further.

The formal point is that we ought to acknowledge the possible tensions between tenacity on the one hand and charity and humility on the other and, in good Aristotelian fashion, teach students to seek a mean between them. No algorithm or procedure can guarantee success in this. Rather, it calls for judgment, and exercising such judgment well is an extremely difficult matter; in fact, it is arguably the defining task of the intellectual life.[22] The best that faculty can do is to conduct ourselves in the classroom, and in our other interactions with students, in ways that model the virtues that we want to communicate to them.

The further point is that at least some of the qualifications needed to pick out virtuous exercises of tenacity from vicious ones seem to be content dependent. That is, whether it is a virtue to hold fast to your views depends, at least in significant part, on what your views are, whether they are admirable or pernicious. Having noticed this about tenacity, we might consider whether an analogous point applies to charity and humility as well. I am inclined to think that it does.

Consider commitments to normative convictions that you find admirable: *respect for human rights is not optional; all people are entitled to equal protection under the law*; and *those in serious need have a claim on our attention and help* all strike me as good candidates. Maybe some students are willing to admit to finding it obvious that counting grass blades is not a good way to spend your life, or that killing a person is indeed worse than killing a bug (no matter what anyone thinks about it). And most have deep commitments to norms of fairness, as a discussion of grading policies can often reveal. I am not concerned about students who cannot be made to doubt these claims in the face of skeptical challenges.

This does not mean that there is no role for rational reflection on these commitments. Often we can helpfully prompt consideration of issues of application, either normative or empirical. For example, we can ask: should we reconceive our assistance to others as owed by justice rather than merely recommended by benevolence? And drawing on the social sciences we can ask: what sorts of attempts at assistance are likely to be most successful in meeting their stated ends? But I am unable to formulate a version of the commitment to the underlying values that calls for intervention. Holding tenaciously to these sorts of commitments, treating them as inevitable, strikes me as a mark of moral maturity.

On the flip side, I am not convinced that the call for charity extends indiscriminately to any view. Intellectual maturity is in part a matter of developing discernment about which views deserve to be taken seriously, a point that becomes clearer as we emphasize the connection between intellectual charity and treating ideas as having the potential to change students' real practical outlooks.[23]

Or consider again Brighouse's claim that the most pressing threat to the autonomy of children and young adults is the consumerism promoted by powerful and well-funded commercial interests. I find focus on this problem helpful, but the content point applies here too: students' tendency toward unreflective materialism, as well as to the subjectivism with which it may be allied, strikes me as problematic not primarily in being unreflective, but rather in being an embrace of bad ideas. Though I'm hopeful that inducing reflection can, at least sometimes, serve to dislodge these ideas, it is their content, not the relation in which students stand to them, that makes them good targets for this. If students leave my classroom embracing these views "for reasons they can articulate," I would not regard this as an educational accomplishment.

The standard version of the autonomy view aims at content neutrality, diagnosing students' problem as standing in a bad relationship to their convictions. I have suggested that the best way to understand autonomy is in terms of the intellectual virtues of charity and humility. Combined with the further point that these virtues, along with tenacity, are relative to the content of the views to which they are applied, this amounts to a significant departure from the standard view, one that abandons a content-neutral picture of intellectual maturity.

Now this might be troubling, because the importance of reflection or critical thinking might have looked like something on which scholars, as such, could be expected to agree. But we know that faculty differ over what constitutes a bad idea that needs to be dislodged and what counts as getting things right. Even the examples I have given, noncontroversial though they are intended to be, will surely call forth some dissent. And of course the more particular the issues we consider and the deeper we go into the particulars of various conceptions of the good, the more disagreement we will encounter. So the thought that it is the content of commitments, more than any formal relation to them, that matters threatens to splinter the aims of the university, with various faculty members working at odds with one another.

I share a sense of discomfort at this prospect, and I don't want to overstate what may seem like a pessimistic conclusion. The scope and depth of the disagreement among faculty, and among thoughtful people generally, should not be overemphasized, nor that of agreement overlooked. I am hopeful that most can endorse the value of the intellectual virtues that I have forwarded and that helping students develop these can be a unifying aim, even if we disagree at the margins about the views to which each is properly applied. Perhaps a somewhat agonistic approach to the matters of disagreement that remain is all right. It may, at any rate, be the best that we can do.[24]

V. Conclusion

I began by claiming that a standard view about educating for autonomy holds that students' primary problem is unreflective or inflexible commitment to some particular conception of the good, often conceived as a traditional view inherited from their families. The standard view holds that the right way to address this problem is to confront the commitments that students have with challenges, provide them with alternatives, and demand that they think critically and give reasons for their commitments. The aim is to make students into autonomous thinkers who can freely choose a conception of the good.

I oppose this picture on all three points. I think that students' most common primary vice is not unreflective traditional commitments, but rather what we might call an overconfident lack of conviction: overconfidence in their negative stance paired with an unwillingness to defend positive normative positions. I speculate that the standard prescription is more likely to exacerbate their problems than to ameliorate them. And I think that the standard prognosis of autonomy is conceptually confused.

Nevertheless, I grant that there is an important truth in the contention that we should aim to make students autonomous, a truth best captured by the intellectual virtues of charity and humility. These virtues themselves require complement by another: the virtue of tenacity. Exercising these virtues appropriately together demands skills of judgment that defy codification. I suggest that none of these virtues can be fully understood apart from the content of the views to which they are applied.

The closest that I have come to prescription is the suggestion that faculty model for students the virtues we ought to be teaching them. This includes modeling good attitudes about both the power and the limits of rational arguments. We ought to communicate both the genuine difficulty of the questions and our own commitments to answers. And we ought to present texts to students not merely as objects to be analyzed and criticized, in a negative sense, but as due positive regard.

Perhaps one of the best things we can do is to display the ideas that we love and try to communicate to students why we love them. This strikes me as standing the best chance of breaking through students' sense that what goes on in the classroom, beyond the mere communication of facts, is irrelevant to their real thought about the world, entertaining at best and downright silly at worst. Unless we can succeed in getting students to connect discussions in the classroom with those outside of it, a liberal education will be hard to justify.

Bibliography

Ackerman, Bruce. 1980. *Social Justice in the Liberal State*. New Haven, CT: Yale University Press.

Bok, Derek. 2007. *Our Underachieving Colleges*. Princeton, NJ: Princeton University Press.

Brandom, Robert. 2000. *Rorty and His Critics*. Malden, MA: Blackwell.

Brighouse, Harry. 2006. *On Education (Thinking in Action)*. New York: Routledge.

Callan, Eamonn. 1997. *Creating Citizens*. New York: Oxford University Press.

Feinberg, Joel. 1980. "The Child's Right to an Open Future." In *Whose Child?*, edited by William Aiken and Hugh LaFollette. Totawa, NJ: Littlefield, Adams.

Foot, Philippa. 1997. "Virtues and Vices." In *Virtue Ethics*, edited by Roger Crisp and Michael Slote. New York: Oxford University Press.

Gutmann, Amy. 1987. *Democratic Education*. Princeton, NJ: Princeton University Press.

Macedo, Stephen. 2000. *Diversity and Distrust*. Cambridge, MA: Harvard University Press.

MacMullen, Ian. 2007. *Faith in Schools?* Princeton, NJ: Princeton University Press.

Nussbaum, Martha. 1997. *Cultivating Humanity*. Cambridge, MA: Harvard University Press.

Powell, Alvin. 2011. "Harvard College Professorships for Five." *Harvard Gazette*, May 12.

Rorty, Richard. 1999. "Education as Socialization and as Individuation." In *Philosophy and Social Hope*, edited by Richard Rorty. New York: Penguin Books.

Smith, Christian. 2011. *Lost in Transition*. New York: Oxford University Press.

Wolterstorff, Nicolas. 2008. *Justice: Rights and Wrongs*. Princeton, NJ: Princeton University Press.

Notes

My thanks to Harry Brighouse, Ian MacMullen, and Alex Tuckness for their feedback on earlier drafts of this chapter, and to Paul Weithman for his formal comments on the version delivered at the conference "The Aims of Higher Education" at Northwestern University.

1. When I talk about the "typical" student I am drawing on my own, admittedly limited, experience. I believe that this experience is representative of what it is like to teach at

a selective university or college, especially in the humanities, and most especially in philosophy. What I have to say may have most relevance in contexts like these, but I hope that it has broader resonance as well.

2. But see, e.g., Ackerman (1980), chapter 5, and Nussbaum (1997), chapters 1 and 2. Some aspects of the view are on display in Brighouse (2006), chapter 1, and Callan (1997), chapters 3 and 6.

3. Powell (2011). The professor quoted is Alison Simmons.

4. See Gutmann (1987), 69: "The risks of democratic and parental tyranny over moral education are reduced (although they can never be eliminated) by providing two substantially separate domains of control over moral education"; also see chapter 2 more generally. And cf. Macedo (2000), 236ff. Macedo writes: "What is crucial from a liberal standpoint is that no one educational authority should totally dominate: that children acquire a measure of distance on all claims to truth in order to be able to think critically about our inclusive political ideals and detect conflicts between those inclusive ideals and their more particular moral and religious convictions" (2000, 238). Also cf. Brighouse (2006), 22: "Autonomy facilitation requires a modicum of discontinuity between the child's home experience and her school experience, so that the opportunities provided by the home (and the public culture) are supplemented, rather than replicated, in the school." Note that all three of these authors are discussing primary and secondary education, rather than higher education, in these passages.

5. It is worth thinking about why this might be. I have several suggestions. First, religious conceptions tend to be better articulated and so better defined than nonreligious conceptions. The major monotheistic religions have central texts, as well as centuries' worth of commentary on these, and many versions have creeds or other doctrinal statements. Of course, these traditions all incorporate a great deal of internal tension and complication, but they are nevertheless better defined than most secular views of the good. The latter are, on the whole, more recent in origin and lacking in institutional structure. This greater development of religious conceptions might be taken to be an obstacle to individual autonomy, discouraging adherents from considering difficult questions one by one. (Though in a later note I will suggest a way in which the opposite might be true.) Second, religious conceptions of the good are relatively widespread in our time and culture. There are many more people who self-conceive as committed to a particular religious view than there are, for example, self-identified utilitarians. This remains true, even while increasing numbers of people identify as areligious or antireligious. A third factor is that religious parents might be particularly concerned with passing down their views to their children. One may occasionally encounter a student whose parents have intentionally raised him in some secular tradition, such as Marxism or comprehensive libertarianism. But students from families concerned to hand down their religious tradition remain far more common, and this might be perceived as a threat to autonomy. Fourth, I think many scholars are in fact moved, some against their official views, by concerns about content and many of these reject religious views. Finally, religious groups are among those most likely to raise legal challenges to educational practices, especially in public schools at the primary and secondary levels. Discussion of education among philosophers and political theorists has been shaped, perhaps too much, by debate about some of these court cases, most prominently *Wisconsin v. Yoder* and *Mozert v. Hawkins*.

6. Nussbaum (1997), 53 and 68.

7. MacMullen has a more developed view than many. He begins with a provisional

characterization of autonomy as capacity for and commitment to critical reflection on one's beliefs (MacMullen 2007, 23), and he rejects as a caricature the conception of autonomy as rational choice uninfluenced by nonrational factors (78). But other aspects of the view seem more in line with the standard conception: "All children should be educated in a way that teaches and encourages them to make their own rational decisions about the good life" (68) and "since we are all born and raised in particular traditions, and none of us is immune to the nonrational appeal of other ways of life, you need to be thoughtful and it helps to be educated if you are to shape and actively endorse your own ethical values rather than merely acquiescing in your family's doctrine" (73).

8. I take the term "feasible option" from Brighouse (2006), 14. Macedo (2000) also holds that it is crucial that "the child is also presented with information about alternative ways of life." He nevertheless rejects the idea that all conceptions of the good should be presented to children neutrally: "The child can rightfully be subjected to parental or public efforts to inculcate their visions of good character" and "both parents and the political community have a right to promote reasonable visions of good character." He does qualify this with the warning that efforts to inculcate a view of the good may not be "repressive" or "seek to indoctrinate." He does not specify the features that distinguish "promotion" from "indoctrination." All quotes are from Macedo (2000), 237. Ackerman (1980) says that the goal of a proper education should be to "provide the child with access to the wide range of cultural materials that he may find useful in developing his own moral ideals and patterns of life," 155–56. And cf. Callan (1997), chapter 6, on "the great sphere," and Feinberg (1980), especially 133 and 139, on children's "right to an open future."

9. See, e.g., Gutmann (1987) and Macedo (2000). See also Brighouse (2006), 92. And cf. MacMullen (2007), chapters 7 and 8: "Schools that aim to initiate children into the practice of autonomous reflection will need deliberately to expose children to diverse and challenging perspectives" (75).

10. Nussbaum (1997), 32. Rorty takes a more adversarial tone than most; see Brandom (2000), 21–22. But Rorty is not an advocate of the standard view, because he makes no claim to content neutrality. Rather he straightforwardly aims to convince students to adopt the views that he thinks are best, using both rational and nonrational means.

11. Bok (2007), 109.

12. Smith (2011).

13. Ibid., 60.

14. Ibid., 21.

15. Ibid., 22.

16. Brighouse (2006), 23. Brighouse also draws attention to a unique and troubling feature of the advocacy of materialist conceptions of the good: those aiming to shape children's values in this way generally do not endorse the views that they aim to inculcate. They have strong financial incentives to spread views that they take to be false; see Brighouse (2006), 50. In spite of his insight on these matters, Brighouse mirrors other contributors to the debate in drawing his paradigmatic examples of potentially heteronomous students from insular traditional religious communities. His discussion, like that of so many, begins with the Amish (2006, 13). In fairness, it should be noted that he distances himself on p. 23 from the idea that the Amish case should be treated as paradigmatic.

17. It's telling then that the Smith study also found that students are astoundingly com-

placent about materialist values. The forces that worry Brighouse have apparently done their work effectively.

18. Students are under other pressures to a subjectivist view as well. Familiar taboos on discussions of religion and politics at family gatherings attest to the difficulty of managing important normative disagreements, especially with people you care about. It is awfully hard to distinguish between disagreement and disrespect when it comes to important matters of value. I think that many students opt to err on the side of suppressing disagreement in order to avoid disrespect, and have been practicing this habit for many years before they enter a college class. These admirable motives tend toward freshman relativism. To complicate matters further, I'm not sure that, at the limits, there is a difference here. Not just any conviction about value is compatible with respect for all. And to complicate matters further still, we can't expect agreement about where this line lies and so when it is crossed.

19. For examples of this rationalist talk see Nussbaum (1997), 9, 33, and 35ff. Though I am not sure how strong Nussbaum means her rationalism to be in the end, the things that she says here suggest that one should endorse only those positions for which one can offer rational justification. For an alternative model of philosophical thought and dialogue see Wolterstorff (2008), xi.

20. Cf. Foot (1997).

21. One could worry that such a student might still lack exposure to alternatives. The student who is completely insulated from all disagreement may indeed lack some good about which autonomy advocates are concerned. But exposure to unfamiliar views isn't itself a virtue of the student. It is, rather, a possible technique for inculcating virtues. So this brings us back to the question I posed earlier: what virtues are we trying to inculcate? Again, I think that charity and humility capture this. Exposure to unfamiliar views probably is necessary for the development of these virtues. Humility conceptually involves awareness that one's own convictions might be wrong, and it's not clear that one could come to this conviction in the complete absence of any alternative. And charity is a virtue that governs the encounter with the unfamiliar. If, as is commonly thought, we develop virtue only through practice, then students need to practice these encounters if they are to have any chance of developing charity.

22. There are grounds for thinking that students who are committed to some traditional conception of the good tend to have a head start in some ways. As I said, I find that they are generally more likely to have given consideration to their outlook, conceived as such. At least some of them are accustomed to dealing with ancient texts and taking these seriously as a possible source of wisdom. Moreover, appreciating the value of a tradition involves awareness that the resources of the tradition almost certainly outstrip your own personal intellectual resources. Thus it involves the idea that you, as an individual, lack complete insight into the most difficult problems and questions. Some students committed to traditional conceptions are obnoxious and blustery, but these aspects of humility are nevertheless often built in to their view.

23. It follows that when we ask students to practice charity toward the views that we present them, we are asking them to trust that we are selecting views worth considering. It seems appropriate to ask this of them, but only if we take our corresponding responsibility seriously.

24. Cf. Rorty (1999) on the ideal social function of colleges.

SIX

Education and Social Moral Epistemology

ALLEN BUCHANAN

Two New Kinds of Knowledge

We are coming to know more about ourselves as knowers. Advances in two areas are of special importance: empirical research about limitations on the ability of cognitively and affectively normal human beings to reason and make judgments, and empirically informed philosophical work that develops the insight that we gain as *social* knowers. The empirical research is occurring in the fields of social psychology, cognitive science, neuroscience, and evolutionary psychology. The philosophical work is in the burgeoning field of social epistemology. As this knowledge develops, our understanding of education should be transformed.

Empirical work on the limitations of the human mind falls under two headings: research on normal lack of capacity and research on normal errors and biases. In both cases, the adjective "normal" signals that the limitations are universal or at least widely distributed among all humans, not just those with cognitive or affective disorders. Research on normal lack of capacity probes psychological or neurological constraints on the ability to process, store, and access large amounts of information, to pursue multiple cognitive tasks simultaneously, and to sustain attention over extended periods of time. Research on normal biases and errors focuses on mistakes in reasoning and judgment. Included under the heading of research on the limitations of the normal human mind is the study of the persistence of cognitive error, in spite of the availability of corrective information.[1]

The second area in which knowledge of ourselves as knowers is increasing is social epistemology, which may be defined as the empirically informed comparative study of the effectiveness and efficiency of alternative social practices, given their tendency to facilitate the formation, transmission, and preservation of true or justified beliefs. In some cases, the social practices studied by social epistemologists are heavily institutionalized, as is the case with contemporary science; in other cases they are more informal, as in the case of ordinary people relying on the testimony of others about which political party to trust or which car to buy.

Social epistemology is grounded in the fact that humans come to know through participation in social practices. The good news, from the standpoint of social epistemology, is that human beings are social knowers and can therefore know much more than they would be able to as isolated individuals. The bad news is that our epistemic dependency makes us vulnerable to systematically mistaken beliefs if our epistemic social practices are defective. By "epistemic social practices" I mean persisting, norm-governed patterns of interaction that affect—for better or worse—our success in forming and sustaining true or justified beliefs.

The Need to Integrate the Two Kinds of Knowledge

For the most part, empirical research on normal limitations of capacity and normal cognitive errors, on the one hand, and social epistemological work, on the other, have been pursued as separate enterprises. That is unfortunate for three reasons. First, some epistemic social practices appear to be ways to cope with the limitations of normal individual minds (science and the social division of labor in its cognitive aspects are two examples). Hence, to understand the functions of such practices and know how effective they are and how they might be improved, it is necessary to understand the cognitive limitations to which they are responses. Thus, social epistemology may need to rely on empirical work on cognitive limitations. Secondly, the *significance* of findings regarding cognitive limitations will depend not only on how serious their consequences are, but also on whether or to what extent either the limitations themselves or their consequences can be mitigated. There is no reason to think that either the extent of our current limitations or their consequences are fixed. Both may vary, depending on our epistemic social practices. So, work in social epistemology may have important implications for the significance of empirical research on normal cognitive limitations. Third, effective strategies for improving human cognition may well require the integration of empirical research on cognitive limitations and social epistemology, in order to pursue complex strategies that combine direct interventions to overcome limitations of the individual mind and new or modified epistemic social practices. (Direct interventions might include learned techniques whereby individuals voluntarily override error-prone cognitive biases as well as biomedical interventions, including pharmaceutical cognitive enhancements and brain-computer interface technologies.) For all of these reasons, empirical research on cognitive limitations and social epistemological work should be mutually informing.

Relevance to Education

Few would deny that research on cognitive limitations has important implications for education. The proximate goal of education is to enable the individual to succeed as a knower, and to do this it is necessary to know what sorts of errors he or she is prone to make and the limits of his or her cognitive capacities. Awareness of predictable cognitive mistakes can inform strategies to avoid or minimize them. For example, if use of the representativeness heuristic results in people's ignoring base rates when making probabilistic judgments, then special efforts should be made to inculcate attention to base rates.[2] Similarly, awareness of our limited capacity to include large numbers of items in our working memory speaks in favor of instructions concerning when to rely on extended-mind strategies, such as computer memory. To take another example, consider the distinction between two types of decision-making processes in cognitively normal individuals. System 1 processes are intuitive and rapid, while system 2 processes are slower, methodical, and rule governed. If, as seems to be the case, many people underutilize system 2 processes for decision making, then, to the extent that activating system 2 processes is within voluntary control, education should teach people techniques for avoiding overreliance on system 1 processes.

The implications of social epistemology for educational practice are less obvious and have received less attention; but, I shall argue, they are equally important, if not more so. My chief aims in the remainder of this paper are to explore some of these implications and to identify obstacles to incorporating into the educational enterprise one especially important aspect of the social epistemological perspective, a critical focus on socially transmitted beliefs that are crucial for moral performance. This subdomain of social epistemology is what I call social moral epistemology.

I. Social Epistemology

A central preoccupation of social epistemology—the novice-expert problem—is clearly relevant to education. We are all novices on many topics, but when there are experts, we can benefit from their expertise, if we can reliably identify them. The problem is, how can someone who lacks knowledge in a certain domain reliably identify those who have knowledge in it? Alvin Goldman's pioneering work, and much of the work that has been stimulated by it, has focused on the novice-expert problem, proposing various heuristics that novices could use in various circumstances to identify genuine experts.[3]

The novice-expert problem is greatly complicated by the fact that the social role of expert carries various benefits (including prestige and earning potential) and opportunities for exploitation (as principal-agent theory shows).[4] The prospect of benefits or opportunities for exploitation can give individuals incentives to signal that they have the expertise they lack. In addition, the motivation needed to enable an individual to bear the costs and risks of developing expertise can sometimes lead the expert to overestimate the extent of his expertise, and this can also result in false, though in this case sincere, signals. (Hence the saying: "For him who has a hammer, everything is a nail.") Novices need strategies to identify experts that take the risk of false signals into account.

Social epistemology can reflect on actual practice to extract generalizable strategies for solving the novice-expert problem. Perhaps the most widely applicable strategy is to use proxies for expertise. For example, if your car mechanic or your physician strenuously resists your proposal to seek a second opinion, that may serve as a proxy for direct evidence of incompetence on their part, just as a used-car dealer's refusal to allow an independent mechanic to inspect the car he wants to sell you can be a proxy for direct evidence of dishonest business practices. Certification or formal credentialing can also serve as a proxy for direct knowledge of an individual's expertise.

Social epistemologists have also illuminated the more general problem of our ubiquitous and unavoidable reliance on the testimony of others. They have developed theories that specify which "acceptance strategies" are appropriate in different testimony environments, using game-theory techniques. Social epistemology is not an alternative to moral psychology or cognitive science. Rather, it draws on those disciplines where relevant, but emphasizes the role of social practices and institutions in believing and knowing.

The Novice-Expert Problem in Education

In education, the novice-expert problem is critical at two levels.[5] First, educators must know how to identify genuine experts in order to determine which information ought to be transmitted to students. In designing science curricula, for example, they must determine which textbooks are scientifically reliable. Secondly, educators should teach students sound strategies for solving the novice-expert problem on their own, in order to increase their chances of cognitive success both in and beyond the classroom. To the extent that social epistemology can identify better solutions to the novice-expert problem, it can make education more effective on both levels.

Here it might be protested that conventional education already teaches people how to respond to the novice-expert problem, even if it doesn't use that phrase. After all, students are taught proper research methods, especially in higher education. That response is not adequate, however. Learning how to identify experts for the purposes of writing an academic research paper is not enough. Most students will not go on to become academics, and even if they do, they will face the novice-expert problem in a variety of venues in which academic research skills will be of limited applicability.

Epistemic Egalitarianism and Epistemic Deference: Striking the Right Balance

As it is usually framed, the novice-expert problem assumes that the novice seeks expert knowledge, that is, that he does not deem him- or herself epistemically adequate in some domain of knowledge. But in some cases, individuals who ought to seek out experts fail to do so, relying excessively on their own cognitive resources. A proper education should inculcate not only strategies for addressing the novice-expert problem, but also the ability to know when one needs to consult experts.

From an epistemic standpoint, a well-designed society is one in which there is a reasonable balance between epistemic egalitarianism and epistemic deference. To make this point clearer, an idealization may be helpful. At one extreme, try to imagine a society of radical epistemic egalitarians, individuals who exhibit no epistemic deference: they always rely on their own views, no matter what the topic. Such a society would be both epistemically and materially impoverished. At the other extreme, try to imagine a society in which everyone suffers from excessive epistemic deference: they automatically defer to putative experts without ever questioning their expertise. The ability of such a society to improve or even to adapt to new challenges in such a way that preserves the status quo would be severely curtailed: no matter how defective its existing patterns of epistemic deference were, they would remain unchallenged.

Two Forms of Epistemic Deference

Status-based epistemic deference exists where individuals defer to others because they recognize them as occupying certain roles, such as physician or clergyman. Merit-based epistemic deference, in contrast, occurs when individuals defer to others because they believe they have independent evidence that others' actual epistemic performance is superior. In a well-designed social practice, identifying an individual as having a certain status is generally a good proxy for their actually performing well epistemically. But in some cases, status is a poor proxy for good epistemic performance. This is true, for example, if status is awarded to those who have certain credentials, but the credentialing process is defective. Where ordinary individuals are generally unable to assess any particular putative expert's epistemic performance directly, status-based deference may be unavoidable, albeit fraught with risk, depending upon how status is awarded. Students should be taught how to distinguish the two forms of epistemic deference and to be able to identify the factors that make status-based deference reasonable, where this includes an understanding of both the benefits and the pitfalls of various types of credentialing systems.

Erosion of Epistemic Deference?

I noted earlier that, from the standpoint of institutional design, the trick is to strike a proper balance between epistemic egalitarianism and epistemic deference. Some believe that in certain domains of knowledge, at least, contemporary American society suffers from excessive epistemic egalitarianism. In particular, they believe that the proper claims of expertise are not being acknowledged on the topic of global climate change.[6] They think that the fact that many Americans do not believe in anthropogenic global climate change indicates a dangerous erosion of epistemic trust in scientific expertise.

Some who deny that there has been anthropogenic global climate change do not question the epistemic capacity of mainstream scientists. Instead, they say that the appropriate exercise of this capacity has been undermined by the liberal ideological commitments that they attribute to the majority of scientists. They believe that mainstream scientists tend to be liberal and that liberals are antibusiness and wish to see a greatly expanded role for government, especially in controlling business. Call this the "liberal corruption theory."

It is not clear, however, that this phenomenon is best characterized as a triumph of epistemic egalitarianism over epistemic deference. An alternative and, perhaps, more plausible characterization is that the belief that mainstream scientists are not trustworthy on the topic of climate change has spread, in part, *because* of epistemic deference: deference to the views of influential conservative pundits, such as Rush Limbaugh, a vocal proponent of the liberal corruption theory. It seems unlikely that thousands of Americans each independently hit upon the liberal corruption theory at roughly the same time. Instead, patterns of epistemic deference seem to have played an important role in the spread of this belief, even if it originated in a number of different conservative minds.

If students reject the claims of scientific experts (whether regarding climate change or evolution), then conventional efforts to teach students how to identify genuine scientific experts will fail in their practical aim: merely identifying experts won't solve the novice-expert problem if one doesn't trust the experts. It is not clear that there is much that educators by themselves can do to prevent misguided distrust of scientists—especially if they, too, are viewed as untrustworthy according to the same liberal corruption theory. Instead, if the problem of lack of trust in scientists is solvable at all, the scientific community, perhaps in cooperation with the media and with government agencies that fund scientific education, may need to make the credentialing of scientists and the processes of conducting research and peer-reviewing submissions for publication more transparent to the general public, in order to make a convincing case that scientific standards are not being undermined by partisan political commitments.[7] The point would not be to try to show that scientists are not subject to biases stemming from their political allegiances, but to explain how the epistemic practices of science can counteract bias.

My aim is not to offer a solution to what I believe to be a dangerous erosion of proper epistemic deference, but only to make two points. First, if education is to fulfill its crucial role of inculcating proper epistemic deference in students, it is not sufficient for educators to reliably identify genuine experts and recommend them to their students. If the social production of status trust has broken down, this will not work. Secondly, whether education can successfully inculcate proper epistemic deference in students may depend not only on what educators do, but also upon the broader social environment, including the actions of other agents, in particular the scientific community itself and government.

The More General Problem: Reducing the Risks
of Social Epistemic Dependency

Improving the student's ability to reliably identify expert sources of information is one way to increase the likelihood that he or she will maximize the benefits of the cognitive division of labor while minimizing the risks. There are other ways, and some are more important for education because the risks they seek to reduce are more serious. I now want to consider a role in education for social epistemology that those who focus on the novice-expert problem or the general problem of testimonial reliability have not discussed. This role is especially important, because the stakes are high. To do so, I must expand on the idea of social *moral* epistemology, briefly introduced above. My aim will be to make the case that in focusing on the novice-expert problem, and the general problem of testimony, social epistemologists have neglected what is arguably the most urgent application of social epistemology to education.

II. Social Moral Epistemology

Morally Crucial Factual Beliefs

Social moral epistemology is that department of social epistemology that focuses on the role of social practices in helping to form, preserve, and transmit those classes of true or justified beliefs that are typically especially important for the well-functioning of our moral powers: our ability to engage in moral reasoning, to make moral judgments, and to experience moral emotions, such as sympathy or a feeling of indignation in the face of injustice.[8]

Depending on the context, almost any factual belief can either enable or undermine the proper functioning of our moral powers. Sometimes a single false belief can result in the commission of a serious moral wrong by a person with morally good intentions and sound moral principles. For example, a policeman who sincerely strives to act on the principle of protecting the innocent may shoot the wrong person because he mistakes an actor being filmed in a street scene for a real criminal about to kill an innocent person. But there are some classes of factual beliefs that typically are especially important for moral performance. This point is most clearly illustrated by negative examples—cases in which various classes of false-factual beliefs tend to undermine moral performance in catastrophic ways. The following four classes of false beliefs seem to play a central role in initiating, or at least sustaining, wrongful mass violence.

1. False beliefs about supposed natural or essential differences between different classes of human beings (e.g., Jews and "Aryans," men and women, blacks and whites).
2. False beliefs about the history of one's nation or ethnic group (e.g., in the case of Germany, that it is the victim of an international Jewish-Bolshevik conspiracy and that in the First World War it was not defeated on the battle-

field but felled by a "stab in the back" from politicians; in the case of Russia, the belief that the explanation for the Chechen secessionist movement is that Chechens are bandits and radical Muslim terrorists, which omits any mention of the well-documented history of Russian oppression in Chechnya and repeated Russian betrayals of autonomy agreements with the Chechen people).

3. False-factual beliefs about the current vulnerability of one's nation or ethnic group. For example, it is reported that when Germany recognized the legitimacy of the Croatian Declaration of Independence in 1992, many Serbs believed that Germany and the new Croatian state would soon cooperate in a genocide against Serbs, on the grounds that Germans and Croatians had done so during World War II. This belief reveals an astonishing ignorance of the difference between the Third Reich and the Germany of 1992, not to mention the equally uninformed assumption that the United States and the other countries of Europe would tolerate another German-perpetrated genocide.

4. False-factual beliefs about (a) the etiology of major social ills (namely, that they were caused by bad genes) and about (b) changes in the human gene pool (namely, that it was rapidly deteriorating), which together led to the false prediction that unless there were rapid and profound changes in human reproductive patterns, there would be a catastrophic decline in the quality of human life and a disintegration of civilization. The combination of these beliefs appears to have motivated or at least helped to sustain compulsory sterilization programs, not just in Nazi Germany, but in liberal constitutional democracies, including Sweden, Denmark, Norway, Canada, and the United States, during the heyday of eugenics.

Social moral epistemology is obviously not just an intriguing intellectual pursuit. It has the potential to improve our moral performance. To the extent that the avoidance of wrongful mass violence is a high moral priority, there is reason to focus special attention on to trying to understand how patterns of epistemic deference contribute to beliefs that play an important role in the etiology of mass violence.

In each of the examples listed above, public education, along with efforts by political elites to exploit other existing mechanisms of epistemic deference in the societies in question (for example, the church and the medical profession), played a significant role in promulgating and sustaining false-factual beliefs that appear to have helped cause large-scale mass violence.

Wrongful mass violence is not limited to genocides, however. Unjust wars are also instances of wrongful mass violence. The public's false beliefs about the rectitude of their own nation and about the behavior and intentions of another nation can make it easier for political leaders to wage unjust war.

Morality in Abeyance or Morality Subverted?

It is useful to distinguish between two different models for understanding how ordinary people—not sociopaths or demons—come to participate in mass wrongful violence. According to the first, moral constraints that ordinary people typically have are overridden or disabled by intense emotion, self-interest, or blind loyalty to leaders. On this view, mass wrongful violence occurs when people's moral values are disconnected from their actions. According to the second model, it is the subversion of moral values, not their impotence, that plays a crucial role in mass wrongful violence. The subversion model captures two disturbing facts about the etiology of mass wrongful violence: first, that for it to occur with widespread participation it is not necessary to expunge or disable conventional moral responses; and secondly, that instead of being generated by amoral or immoral motives, it can in fact be morally motivated.[9] In brief, on the subversion model, the instigators of mass wrongful violence do not so much disable people's moral motivation as redirect it toward immoral ends. They typically do this by facilitating the promulgation of morally crucial false-factual beliefs, usually beliefs of the sort listed above. When they do this successfully, it is because they exploit the existing patterns of epistemic deference that are embedded in key social practices and institutions. They may also exploit normal cognitive biases, including the tendency to sort human beings into supposedly natural kinds, defined by unchanging essences that rigidly determine behavior. On some accounts, racist thinking and ethnonational stereotypes are specific instances of an evolved tendency toward such essentialist thinking.[10]

What is darkly fascinating about these cases of socially transmitted false-factual beliefs is that they enable the subversion of morality without any major change in basic moral principles. Consider the first item in the list. Nazi propaganda embedded the distinction between Jews and "Aryans" in a web of false beliefs about natural differences, along with a false view of history in which a supposed Jewish-Bolshevik conspiracy was a major factor. Jews were presented as subhuman, crafty, and deadly vermin who, unless exterminated, would enslave the German nation and destroy Western civilization. If one believed all this to be true, then one could see the rightness of the extermination of the Jews without abandoning any fundamental conventional moral principles. After all, conventional morality recognizes a right of self-defense against lethal, wrongful threats. Similarly, one can sustain one's commitment to the Golden Rule if one thinks that it applies only to persons and that Jews (or blacks, or Croats) are not persons because by nature they lack some of the necessary features of personhood.[11]

Another example illustrates how false-factual beliefs about "natural" differences among classes of human beings can be invoked to perpetuate patent injustices, even if they do not rise to the level of genocide. In countries where Muslim doctrines strongly influence the shape of the legal system, women are not allowed to give evidence in court in some types of cases, and when they are allowed, their testimony sometimes does not count as much as that of men. The explicit justification given for this discriminatory practice is that women by their nature are not as reliable witnesses as men because they are excessively emotional and have an inferior knowledge of the world.[12] This example illustrates a feature of unjust social practices generally, including those that involve discrimination on grounds of color or gender: namely, that the justification given for them typically relies on false-factual claims about supposed natural differences—claims that are not supported by empirical evidence but are nonetheless effectively transmitted and sustained by patterns of epistemic deference.

To summarize, the key point is that individuals who have undergone what we now regard as successful moral development are nonetheless vulnerable to the subversion of their moral powers by socially inculcated false-factual beliefs through the operation of social practices that include patterns of epistemic deference. Further, we have unfortunately had enough experience with the subversion of morality to be able to identify certain classes of false-factual beliefs as being especially dangerous. These include beliefs about "natural" differences that are thought to be relevant to judgments of moral status or civil rights, beliefs about the past victimization or current vulnerability of one's nation or ethnic group, and beliefs about the supposed biological causes of social ills and predictions of catastrophic biological degeneration. Finally, we know that these classes of especially morally dangerous false-factual beliefs are typically promulgated through existing mechanisms of epistemic deference embodied in various social practices and roles—and that educational institutions have often played a role in their promulgation. This gives us good reason to prioritize what might be called negative or preventative social moral epistemology in our efforts to incorporate the insights of social epistemology into educational practices, focusing first and foremost on those types of beliefs that tend to contribute to mass wrongful violence.

So far, I have dwelled only on the moral risk we all run as a result of two factors: our social epistemic dependency and the fact that false beliefs can subvert our moral powers. The same two factors also create a profound prudential risk: through misplaced epistemic deference, we may come to have false-factual beliefs that lead us to act in ways that severely damage our own interests. The tremendous human and material losses suffered by the German people as a result of their support for the Nazi program of extermination and conquest is an obvious example, but there are many others.

Social moral epistemology is concerned with the social transmission of any beliefs that tend to compromise our moral performance, not just with those that contribute to wrongful mass violence. As Jonathan Glover has argued, however, the history of the last century gives us reason to focus special efforts on avoiding the worst moral wrongs.[13] My point is not that educational practices should focus only on beliefs that contribute to mass wrongful violence but rather that such beliefs should receive special scrutiny.

Two Ways Social Practices Can Foster Risky Factual Beliefs

Sometimes social practices inculcate morally or prudentially damaging false-factual beliefs by explicitly teaching them. But in other cases, social practices encourage the formation of such beliefs by creating a distorted social experience that fosters the formation of false beliefs. Consider, for example, a society characterized by deeply entrenched sexist practices that systematically exclude women from a wide range of opportunities in education, business, and politics. The experience of all members of such a society, men as well as women, will be systematically distorted. In particular, no one will have an opportunity to gather reliable evidence about the "natural" capacities of women because sex discrimination will systematically prevent women from developing and freely exercising their capacities. Growing up in a society in which women are never given the opportunity to become educated or to excel in business or politics, one may incorrectly come to believe that women are less capable in these respects than men.

Recall the Islamic jurists' rationale for discounting women's testimony: women are said to be too inexperienced in the ways of the world—and this in a society in which the disallowing of their legal testimony is one element in a web of discrimination that systematically prevents them from full participation in the world that they are then said to be constitutionally incapable of comprehending. If education is to take social moral epistemology seriously, it must make students aware not only of the risk of misplaced epistemic deference in the case of beliefs that are explicitly inculcated, but also of the fact that their morally crucial beliefs can be systematically distorted by the very social practices which those same beliefs are invoked to justify, quite apart from any explicit teaching of falsehoods.

Public Education, Patriotic Bias, and War

Public education has never had education as its sole function. Historically, public education has played a significant role in turning children into citizens and in "nation building," which has usually involved falsification of the nation's historical record.[14] Only in the last few decades, and then only in some countries, have serious efforts been made by public educators to ensure that textbooks convey an accurate, impartial understanding of history and the nation's role in it.[15] To the extent that a biased presentation of history is transmitted to students, it predisposes them to erroneous judgments that are both morally and prudentially risky. For example, a distorted view of the motives and consequences of U.S. military interventions over the last 175 years will tend, other things being equal, to make citizens less likely to take seriously the moral and prudential risks of the next proposed intervention. How optimistic an individual will be about the good to be achieved by a proposed U.S. military intervention in Iraq may depend upon whether the history textbook he or she read in high school explained the deception perpetrated by the Johnson administration regarding the Gulf of Tonkin incident and made it clear that although the My Lai massacre was apparently the worst case of a war crime committed by U.S. soldiers in Vietnam, it was not the only one.

Similarly, textbooks and films (both documentary and fictional) that exaggerate the role of the United States in defeating Nazi Germany (while grossly underplaying the far greater role of the Soviet Union) may contribute to an ill-founded sense of military invulnerability and to the belief that the rest of the world, especially "the Europeans," is not sufficiently grateful to the United States for having vanquished the Nazis.[16] Delusions of military invulnerability and a misplaced sense of resentment at supposed ingratitude may, in turn, bias citizens' decisions to support the use of military power or to do so unilaterally, in the face of opposition from the supposedly ungrateful countries. In countries in which textbooks are still seriously biased, taking the perspective of social moral epistemology can motivate and guide efforts to reduce bias. In countries in which reform has already occurred, it can help ensure that students are equipped by their education to resist adopting distorted beliefs conveyed by other institutions, including government, the mainstream media, and social media. This second function of an education informed by social moral epistemology is especially important in an era in which the role of education in belief formation may be eclipsed by the role of electronic media.

The threads of the argument so far can now be tied together. Educational policy should not only take social epistemology seriously because the success of the educational enterprise requires an effective response to two of the central problems of social epistemology, namely, the novice-expert problem and the general problem of identifying reliable testimony. In addition, social *moral* epistemology is especially relevant to education for two additional reasons. First, if education is informed by social moral epistemology, it can play a protective or preventative role, by providing critical skills and sound historical information that can reduce the risk that their beliefs will be manipulated by political leaders and others who mobilize the public in support of wrongful mass violence. Second, the critical tools of social moral epistemology can help those who design or oversee the educational enterprise to prevent it from being a contributor to the production of false beliefs that tend to support mass violence.

In order to help students avoid the moral and prudential risks of our epistemic dependency, education will have to first become much more self-critical, taking to heart the central insights of social moral epistemology. Educators will have to apply the critical tool of social moral epistemology to themselves and the epistemic practices they create.

Why Teaching Critical Thinking Is Not Enough

Some educators might respond with indignation to the analysis thus far. They might point out that education, at least in democratic countries, has become more self-critical and in doing so has enlarged its understanding of what skills students need. In particular, they might cite efforts to introduce courses in critical thinking into the curriculum.

The difficulty with this response is that critical thinking, as it is conventionally conceived, fails to take the insights of social epistemology seriously. Critical-thinking texts typically focus on teaching students to critique arguments, that is, to understand which inferences from an assumed set of premises are valid and which are not. In some cases they also teach elementary probabilistic reasoning; but they typically do not focus sufficiently on the problem of determining whether the premises in arguments are true or justified. Nor do they emphasize our ineliminable reliance on testimony from others (broadly understood) and the risks it entails. Finally, critical-thinking texts tend to omit the novice-expert problem altogether. In short, they proceed as if the knower operated as an isolated individual whose problem is not to identify correct information but to reason correctly on the basis of information assumed to be correct.[17]

A more satisfactory approach would be to rethink the subject matter of critical-thinking courses in the light of social moral epistemology. And to the extent that the avoidance of wrongful mass violence should be a social priority, a new approach to critical thinking should include a special emphasis on making students more critically aware of those classes of beliefs that can do the most moral damage. In brief, social moral epistemology, especially in its negative or preventative form, should be a major factor in the design of critical-thinking texts and curricula.

The Inadequacy of the Millian Response

I have argued elsewhere that, other things being equal, societies in liberal constitutional democracies are more likely to have better epistemic social practices, in part because there will be more opportunities for detecting and correcting practices that involve misplaced epistemic deference.[18] It would be a mistake, however, to conclude from this that what I shall call the Millian solution is an adequate response to the moral and prudential risks of our social epistemic dependency. The Millian solution is to support a "free market of ideas" within a framework of liberal constitutional democracy in order to foster freedom of expression in the expectation that over the long run, at least, true or justified beliefs will predominate—or, at least, that the most dangerous beliefs will be exposed and corrected.

The main problem with the Millian solution is that it relies on a picture of the individual knower that completely overlooks both the findings of empirical research on the limitations of the human mind and the insights of social epistemology. Individual knowers, as we have seen, suffer a number of normal cognitive limitations and are prone to a variety of cognitive errors. Although social epistemic practices may sometimes mitigate these limitations or correct for these errors, they can and frequently do introduce distortions of their own. Simply allowing the maximal production and free dissemination of information will not solve either of these problems. Even when excellent information is available, individuals may either fail to become aware of it because it is not endorsed by those to whom they accord epistemic deference or discount it because it clashes with beliefs or patterns of action to which they are already committed (exhibiting confirmation bias or otherwise resolving cognitive dissonance in epistemically flawed ways). It is worth remembering that the contagion of morally damaging eugenic thinking occurred in liberal democratic societies with commendable freedom of expression.[19]

The situation of the human knower is not that of a perfectly rational being in direct contact with the full array of relevant information, with each bit of information having the same salience until the knower rationally attaches a probability to it through judicious adherence to sound evidentiary norms. It is that of a being with flawed and limited cognitive faculties who is aware of only a fraction of the available information, with the bits of information he or she is aware of already endowed with epistemic weights attached through the mediation of defective social epistemic practices that subject him or her to moral and prudential risks to which he or she is largely oblivious. Which of these radically different images of the knower one assumes makes a great difference to how one ought to conceive the educational enterprise.

III. Objections and Obstacles

How Important Are Beliefs?

So far I have argued for the integration of empirical research on the limitations of the normal human mind with the insights of social epistemology and recommended that educational institutions take to heart the fruits of this collaboration. I have also argued that in addition to conveying to students the seriousness and ubiquity of the novice-expert problem and providing them with information about the best strategies for addressing it, educational institutions should make social moral epistemology a priority. For example, through the use of well-documented historical case studies (such as that of the eugenics movement and the racial ideologies that supported slavery, segregation, and genocide), educators should teach students to be especially critical of certain classes of beliefs—namely, those that have repeatedly played a role in initiating and sustaining wrongful mass violence or patent injustices.

The case for incorporating social moral epistemology into education obviously rests on the assumption that false beliefs play a significant role in the etiology of wrongful mass violence. As commonsensical as this assumption will appear to most, it appears to be challenged by some recent empirical psychological research and by some empirically informed philosophical theorizing about the relationship between moral responses and the emotions. In brief, this work might be seen as undermining the assumption that moral responses are sensitive to changes in belief—as well as my claim that empirical research on cognitive limitations and work in social epistemology are complementary rather than antagonistic.

It is beyond the scope of this essay to provide a critical survey of the expanding domain of empirical work on morality and the emotions. Instead, I will only sketch briefly the positions of two influential thinkers, John Haidt and Jesse Prinz, that might be thought to cast serious doubt on the fundamental assumptions of social moral epistemology.

In a now famous experiment, Haidt asked members of an undergraduate class whether they thought incest between brothers and sisters was wrong. Most said it was wrong, without hesitation. He then asked them why it was wrong.[20] For each answer given, Haidt filled in details of the example to vitiate the objection (for example, to allay worries of genetically defective offspring, he specified that there was no chance of conception). Haidt reports that even when every reason against incest in the case specified had been rendered irrelevant, the students persisted in their judgment that the behavior was wrong. From this he concludes that moral response (or judgment) is emotional and not responsive to reasoning.

Haidt's overinterpretation of his meager data is breathtaking. If, as one would assume, the moral norm against incest is a deeply entrenched one, then one should not expect that it will be successfully expurgated through the brief sort of discursive exercise that occurs in the experiment. In fact, it is hard to see how basic moral norms, if they could be abandoned this easily, could perform the fundamental role that they do in coordinating behavior. Moreover, one would think that part of what makes basic moral norms resilient in the face of challenges is that they are strongly supported by social practices of epistemic deference. But if that is so, then it seems even less likely that a few minutes' discussion in a classroom would overturn them (unless one has a wildly inflated view of the status trust accorded to professors in our society). Further, even if Haidt is right that moral judgments are not responsive to changes in belief once the corresponding moral norms have become entrenched in the individual's psyche, this is fully consistent with the notion that belief plays an important role in the initial formation of moral responses.

Prinz has a much more philosophically sophisticated and better developed moral psychology.[21] He advances the bold claim that moral judgments are just emotions. In fact, he seems to be committed to the view that all moral responses are a particular emotion, or a very small set of emotions, something akin to disgust or in some cases something like a combination of disgust and anger.

One obvious objection to this view is that there are many types of moral judgments, and Prinz is committed to the very counterintuitive claim that what differentiates various types of moral judgments is something wholly external to them. According to him, there are various rules whose cognitive activation causes the emotional response. But suppose one sets aside the counterintuitiveness of the claim that moral judgments as different as *that is unjust* and *that is ungenerous* are really just expressions of the same emotion, distinguished only by the fact that they are triggered by the application of different rules external to them. The point is that once we become conscious of the rules whose activation triggers the emotions that are moral judgments, it appears that we are in a position to evaluate the rules, and that how we evaluate them can depend on what beliefs we have—about what generosity or justice is, what its effects are, and so on. So, even if we accept Prinz's claim that moral judgments are just emotions, it does not follow that moral judgments are not sensitive to changes in beliefs.

There are two ways to support social moral epistemology's assumption that morally crucial false-factual claims typically play an important role in wrongful mass violence. The first is to argue, as I have just done, that empirical findings or empirically informed philosophical theories that purport to undermine this assumption fail to do so. The second is to proceed empirically, documenting the fact that successful instigators of wrongful mass violence invariably prepare the ground for atrocities by trying to instill false-factual beliefs that, if combined with largely unexceptionable moral principles, justify horrible actions. In brief, relying on historical cases, one can argue that successful instigators of wrongful mass violence are employing a folk psychology that is accurate enough to work for their purposes. Absent convincing evidence that, contrary to appearances, false beliefs do not play a significant role in wrongful mass violence (and thus that those whom we regard as masters of murderous propaganda are really deluded and utterly impotent), it seems plausible to conclude that what appears to be the case is so: false-factual beliefs of the sort listed above typically do play some significant role in initiating, or at least in sustaining, wrongful mass violence.

More positively, a plausible case can be made that the reduction of wrongful mass violence has sometimes been successfully achieved by strategies in which the correction of morally crucial false-factual beliefs appears to have been an important factor. One of the best documented cases of this sort is the British abolitionist movement. Abolitionists pursued a sophisticated strategy of social and political mobilization in which efforts to change people's beliefs played a significant role. These beliefs were of several sorts. First, there were those having to do with the supposed natural characteristics of Africans, in particular the belief that they were not rational beings. Second, there were beliefs about their capacity for suffering and for well-being, in particular the belief that being enslaved did not cause them extreme suffering and that they were comparatively happy in their servitude. Third, there were beliefs about the effects of the slave trade on others. In particular, the abolitionists went to great lengths to provide evidence that the slave trade had a negative impact on the well-being of sailors working on ships that transported slaves.[22] In all of these respects, their remarkably successful strategy was premised on the assumption that false-factual beliefs help sustain immoral behavior, whether they play a significant role in originating it or not. Similarly, for some people at least, learning about the horrific conditions under which animals are raised and slaughtered for food, when combined with scientifically backed information about their capacity for suffering, seems to change not only their moral judgments, but their behavior as well.

Obstacles

In my judgment, there are three main obstacles to reshaping education in the light of what social moral epistemology can teach us. First, there is the apparently widespread, if not universal, tendency of people to underestimate their epistemic dependency. We tend to think of ourselves as much more independent—and much more rational—in forming and sustaining our beliefs than we in fact are.[23] Until this delusion is dispelled, it will be difficult to convince people that education should take social moral epistemology seriously. Secondly, there is the fact that both conventional morality and philosophical ethics have failed to appreciate the centrality of the ethics of believing to the moral life. Given how much of our behavior depends on our beliefs, there is surprisingly little emphasis on the epistemic virtues of individuals—or, rather, on the crucial dependence of our moral performance on our epistemic performance. So, rethinking education in the light of social moral epistemology may first require rethinking morality. Thirdly, too many people confuse patriotism with participation in a conspiracy of silence, a refusal to acknowledge, at least in public and especially in politics, that one's own country has done wrong. This tendency is all too apparent in the ferocious political opposition to even the most anemic attempts to rewrite public-school American history textbooks in a less drastically partial fashion. Most of us would agree, I think, that an individual who is incapable of admitting that he has done wrong is far from virtuous—he is either a sociopath, a knave, a fool, or a coward. Yet many of us tend to think that such denial is appropriate at the collective level.

My surmise is that it is the vice of cowardice that predominates among those who regard criticism of one's own country as unpatriotic. Perhaps at some level they fear that their commitment to their country or their sense of their own worth as belonging to that country will dissipate in the cold light of the truth. Alternatively, some people may shrink from acknowledging their country's faults because they fear that doing so will result in a disastrous loss of support for the country. This prediction, ironically, seems to betray a rather low estimation of one's country's merits and their ability to command solidarity.

Regardless of which diagnosis of the psychological roots of this phenomenon is correct, the fact is that many people apparently think that not admitting one's country's errors is an important constituent of the virtue of patriotism. Such people may be in the thrall of a factual belief that is on the face of it quite implausible, or at the very least not adequately supported by evidence: namely, that a society cannot flourish unless it systematically lies about its own character. Although I know of no evidence that societies that acknowledge collective errors disintegrate, I do know that there is evidence that admission of collective error does not cause fatal social disruption. Germany's sustained effort to acknowledge and come to grips with the horrors of the Third Reich is one commendable example.[24] Others include countries such as South Africa, where truth and reconciliation processes do not appear to have torn the social fabric but may even have helped heal potentially dangerous wounds.

Conclusions

I have argued that education should be reshaped in the light of our growing knowledge of our limitations as knowers. The educational enterprise should take to heart two growing bodies of knowledge: empirical research on the limitations of normal cognition and work in social epistemology that emphasizes both the benefits and the risks of our social epistemic dependency. Finally, I have also argued that, given the seriousness of the problem of wrongful mass violence, there is a strong case for reshaping education in the light of the basic insights of social moral epistemology, focusing critical attention on the role of social practices in inculcating, spreading, and preserving those classes of false-factual beliefs that tend to carry the greatest moral and prudential risks.

Notes

I wish to thank Russell Powell for his research assistance in preparing this paper and the Spencer Foundation for funding his work. I am also grateful to Greg Robson for research assistance and indebted to Harvey Seigal for valuable comments.

1. In some cases, heuristics appear to be adaptations to cope with cognitive limitations.
2. To use the representativeness heuristic is to judge the probability that a given indi-

vidual is an X (e.g., an accountant as opposed to a bus driver or a policeman) on the basis of the fact that the individual has characteristics normally associated with being an X, without taking into account how frequent the occurrence of Xs (as opposed to Ys or Zs, for instance) is in the population, thus ignoring base rates.

3. Alvin I. Goldman, *Knowledge in a Social World* (Oxford: Oxford University Press, 1999).

4. For an exploration of the extent to which principal-agent theory can be fruitfully used in social epistemology, see Allen Buchanan, "Principal/Agent Theory and Social Epistemology," unpublished paper.

5. Goldman, *Knowledge in a Social World*, briefly discusses the novice-expert problem in the context of education in his final chapter, where he also defends his veritistic social epistemology against postmodernist views of education.

6. Similarly, surveys indicating that 30 percent of Americans believe the earth to be less than ten thousand years old suggest that there is a massive failure to appreciate the expertise of Darwinian evolutionary biologists.

7. Philip Kitcher suggests that what is needed is a new social practice in which representatives of the general public are tutored by scientists, giving them something more like an insider's view of how science works. Philip Kitcher, *Science in a Democratic Society* (Amherst, NY: Prometheus Books, 2011). I am skeptical that such an arrangement would work under the very conditions of distrust of mainstream science it is designed to address. Those who are skeptical of mainstream science are not likely to trust the tutoring process, and the effort to include representatives of the general citizenry might result in some individuals participating in the process only to wreck it or use it as a stage for political theater.

8. For development of the idea of social moral epistemology, see Allen Buchanan, "Social Moral Epistemology and the Tasks of Ethics," in *Ethics and Humanity: Themes from the Philosophy of Jonathan Glover*, ed. N. Ann Davis, Richard Keshen, and Jeff McMahan (Oxford: Oxford University Press, 2010), and "Political Liberalism and Social Epistemology," *Philosophy and Public Affairs* 32, no. 2 (2004): 95–130.

9. For example, the historian Claudia Koonz makes a strong case that participation in Nazi atrocities was often morally motivated and that Nazi indoctrination, especially of the SS, involved the inculcation of very demanding, albeit subverted, morality. Claudia Koonz, *The Nazi Conscience* (Cambridge, MA: Belknap Press of the Harvard University Press, 2003), especially 26–130.

10. Lawrence A. Hirschfeld, *Race in the Making: Cognition, Culture, and the Child's Construction of Human Kinds* (Cambridge, MA: MIT Press, 1996); and David Livingstone Smith, *Less than Human: Why We Demean, Enslave, and Exterminate Others* (New York: St. Martin's Press, 2011).

11. Smith, *Less than Human*, 119; see also Hirschfeld, *Race in the Making*.

12. Scott C. Lucas, "Justifying Gender Inequality in the Shafi'i Law School: Two Case Studies of Muslim Legal Reasoning," *Journal of the American Oriental Society* 129, no. 2 (2009): 237–58.

13. Jonathan Glover, *Humanity: A Moral History of the Twentieth Century* (New Haven, CT: Yale University Press, 2000).

14. Eugen Weber, *Peasants into Frenchmen* (Stanford, CA: Stanford University Press, 1976). For a fascinating study of how popular American public-school history textbooks falsify history, see James W. Loewen, *Lies My Teacher Told Me: Everything Your American History Textbook Got Wrong* (New York: Simon & Schuster, 2007).

15. For a history of the so-called culture wars debate about revisions of public-school

history texts in the United States, see Gary Nash, Charlotte Crabtree, and Ross Dunn, *History on Trial: Culture Wars and the Teaching of the Past* (New York: Knopf, 1997). For a fascinating study of how American public-school history textbooks have been revised in response to changes in the political and cultural context, see Frances Fitzgerald, *America Revised: History Schoolbooks in the Twentieth Century* (Boston: Little, Brown, 1979). Fitzgerald's book, like Loewen's, documents how history textbooks commonly promote values such as "citizenship" and "patriotism" and fuel dubious beliefs in American exceptionalism at the expense of truth.

16. Norman Davies documents the extent of the popular misconception in America and Great Britain of the relative contributions of the Western Allies and the Soviet Union toward the defeat of the Third Reich. Norman Davies, *No Simple Victory: World War II in Europe, 1939–1945* (New York: Viking Press, 2007).

17. There are exceptions—critical-thinking texts that are more congenial to a social-epistemology approach—including Richard Feldman, *Reason and Argument*, 2nd ed. (Upper Saddle River, NJ: Prentice Hall, 1999); and Trudy Govier, *A Practical Study of Argument*, 4th ed. (Belmont, CA: Wadsworth, 1997).

18. Buchanan, "Political Liberalism and Social Epistemology."

19. For an application of the idea of social moral epistemology to the eugenics movements in liberal democratic countries, see Allen Buchanan, "Institutions, Beliefs, and Ethics: Eugenics as a Case Study," *Journal of Political Philosophy* 15, no. 1 (2007): 22–45.

20. John Haidt, "The Emotional Dog and Its Rational Tail: A Social Intuitionist Approach to Moral Judgment," *Psychological Review* 108, no. 4 (2001): 814–34.

21. Jesse Prinz, *The Emotional Construction of Morals* (Oxford: Oxford University Press, 2007); *Reactions: A Perceptual Theory of Emotion* (New York: New York University Press, 2004); and *Furnishing the Mind: Concepts and Their Perceptual Basis* (Cambridge, MA: MIT Press, 2004).

22. Adam Hochschild, *Bury the Chains: Prophets and Rebels in the Fight to Free an Empire's Slaves* (New York: Houghton Mifflin, 2005).

23. Allen Buchanan, "Social Moral Epistemology," *Social Philosophy and Policy* 19, no. 2 (2002): 126–52.

24. The dogmatic belief that a country cannot thrive under conditions of public honesty may be only one application of a more general article of faith that is common in conservative thinking: the steadfast but remarkably underevidenced belief that society is a fragile, seamless web that can remain intact only if most people unthinkingly comply with social norms, rarely if ever questioning authority, and if the actual functionings of the social order are not subjected to conscious scrutiny by many people.

SEVEN

Righting Historical Injustice
in Higher Education

LIONEL K. MCPHERSON

I

Mainstream institutions of higher education, which in the United States have a dominant orientation that is white and secular, are often thought of as "liberal" bastions. The liberal ideal can be identified with a belief in the moral and political equality of persons, regardless of gender, color, creed, or nationality; a commitment to reason-based methods of inquiry and argument; intellectual and creative independence from religious and political authority; and concern about fairness and socioeconomic inequality, in contrast to sheer self-interest. After the social upheavals of the 1960s, mainstream higher education came to be viewed as a site for progressive change—even if anyone who has spent time on campuses over the last twenty-five years can confirm that they are not a breeding ground for radicalism. Yet we can safely say that professors and students are more liberal than Americans overall.[1]

At the same time, mainstream institutions of higher education have hardly led the way regarding racial justice. This claim runs counter to popular perception: with affirmative action for black Americans always under scrutiny, academia is seen as trying to make racial progress a priority, for better or worse. Such a perception is misguided. Mainstream higher education enabled practices of discrimination against blacks, the consequences of which continue to shape racialized inequality in our society. Historically white colleges and universities have largely failed to acknowledge, let alone to rectify, their complicity in racial injustice. In an era celebrated for approximating a postracial state of affairs, these institutions have a corrective responsibility toward black Americans that is as urgent as ever in recent memory. The purpose of talk of responsibility here is neither to assign backward-looking blame nor to shift all burden of decreasing racialized inequality away from blacks themselves. Rather, I will make a case for forward-looking action on behalf of a racially just society in general and racially just higher education in particular—a case that rests on the legacy of antiblack racial injustice, including in the domain of higher education.

II

A distinction is made in political philosophy between ideal theory and nonideal theory. The assumption driving ideal theory is that members of a society can arrive at and abide by principles for the just arrangement of social and political institutions. Ideal theory thus delivers a model whereby the principles of justice are not influenced by plain irrationality, selfishness, indifference, and the like—factors that would undermine the implementation or effectiveness of the principles.[2] By contrast, nonideal theory responds to practical obstacles to justice such as lack of compliance, absence of political will, inadequate resources, and legacies of past injustice. Nonideal theory thus can license departures from what principles of ideal theory would require. For instance, ideal theory would hold that individuals should not be benefited or burdened on account of their racial identity. But nonideal theory might allow that when a social group has been unjustly burdened or has unjustly benefited on account of racial identity, race-conscious polices should be enacted that would help to offset the unfair distribution of burdens and benefits.

I do not dismiss the value of ideal theory, which can provide fundamental guidance about the targets of justice. Equality of opportunity is one such target. The political liberalism that John Rawls famously elaborated, for example, supports substantive and not merely formal equality of opportunity. Yet the Rawlsian tradition of ideal theorizing has been uncomfortably quiet about the realities of a racialized society.[3] So I will leave ideal theory behind in the background in thinking about the connection between race and education in the United States. While I favor a politically liberal approach to justice, with its emphasis on a roughly egalitarian distribution of resources and opportunities, my argument here is not especially tied to political liberalism. Nor am I directly arguing for the priority of corrective (racial) justice over distributive justice. These approaches to justice are initiated at different levels—the nonideal and the ideal, respectively.

If everyone suddenly had what distributive justice assigns them, questions of corrective justice would be rendered moot: ideal principles would indeed have been actualized. To acknowledge this, though, is not to accept the notion that we would do better to stop worrying about the racially unjust past and instead aim for distributive justice in the present. In ideal theory and in actual practice, distributive justice can be not unreasonably contested. Distributive justice, in any event, will not be taking effect in the United States in the foreseeable future. Meanwhile there is an important role for corrective justice.

My narrower concern for corrective racial justice is relatively freestanding. No commitment to distributive justice is needed in order to recognize that corrective measures should be taken to address the unfavorable circumstances of a social group that continues to be substantially burdened by a history of injustice. Moreover, the notion that aiming for distributive justice—whatever this might involve in a society that by and large disavows such a conception of justice—is somehow at odds with or indifferent to pursuing corrective justice strikes me as bizarre.[4] The fact that many persons seem tired of hearing about the legacy of racial injustice and possible measures to correct it is not a compelling rationale for ending the discussion. In short, a concern for corrective racial justice operates at the level of nonideal theory and is compatible with more general conceptions of justice initiated at the level of ideal theory.

The problem, as I will formulate it, is doubly nonideal: the United States remains highly racialized de facto, yet we are living at a time when popular and political desire to deal with this reality is weak. The operative question is not whether we can imagine the form that corrective policies could take, but, rather, whether we can develop corrective practices that would not have to rely on popular and political support. For this reason, I mainly will have in mind private institutions of higher education, where public backing is not necessarily a condition for promoting racial justice. The University of Michigan, for instance, saw Supreme Court rulings that permitted "narrowly tailored" affirmative action programs—via *Grutter v. Bollinger* (2003) and *Gratz v. Bollinger* (2003)—trumped when in 2006 Michigan voters passed Proposal 2, which banned public affirmative action altogether. While states— for example, California, whose voters passed the anti–affirmative action Proposition 209 (1996)—might partially restore the effects of banned race-conscious policies through ostensibly race-neutral means, this is beside the point of the argument I will make. My aim in looking to private institutions of higher education is not to subvert democratic processes. It is to work around formidable majoritarian or legalistic barriers to corrective justice practices.

The United States is close to becoming legally postracial, even as evidence suggests that ostensibly race-neutral schemes often will prove far less effective than race-conscious policies that are supposed to benefit blacks.[5] By legally postracial, I mean that racial discrimination is prohibited in the public sphere and also that racial identities are presumed by law to be irrelevant there. A legally postracial society is compatible with a society that is not socially postracial. Some proponents of legal postracialism are undisturbed by this possibility, since they cite—whether as a matter of constitutional or moral principle—an overriding commitment to color blindness in law's domain at this point in history.

Other proponents of legal postracialism suggest that public color blindness happens to be the best way now or soon of achieving racial progress. These more pragmatic proponents can allow that while the law should move strongly in a color-blind direction, a very limited role for race-conscious policies might be appropriate for a limited time longer. Supreme Court Justice Sandra Day O'Connor, for instance, wrote in her majority opinion in the *Grutter* case, "We expect that 25 years from now, the use of racial preferences will no longer be necessary to further the interest approved today [viz., the educational benefits of racial diversity]."[6] This type of gesture toward legal postracialism, though, sidesteps principled debate about the basis for limiting corrective race-conscious policies in time or scope. After all, few would deny that other things being equal, a legally postracial society is a more just society. Race-conscious policies obviously are supposed to be a response to unequal and unjust circumstances.

The notion that the United States is becoming socially postracial—with persons no longer treating race as a factor in their lives or, at least, with race no longer a useful proxy for patterns of social inequality—represents a certain aspiration more than a reality. O'Connor has recognized as much after retiring from the Court: troubled by the persistent racial achievement gap in primary and secondary education, she clarifies that her "25-year expectation is, of course, far from binding on any justices who may be responsible for entertaining a challenge to an affirmative action program in 2028," since she takes the legal task to involve "applying abstract constitutional principles to concrete education endeavors."[7] More broadly, racial identity still tracks profound disparities in income, family wealth, health, and education, with blacks on average continuing to do much worse than whites; and black Americans continue to experience a high degree of residential segregation.[8] Formal mechanisms of law and niceties of public discourse about race have left a racialized society intact. Whatever the explanations, the persistent significance of racial identity in the United States cannot be denied.

The distinction between a legally postracial society and a socially post-racial one helps to highlight a challenge to positive change. If racial identities still matter in ways beyond the policing of overt discrimination in the public sphere, then we will want to take seriously the possibility that racial inequalities in education are unlikely to be rectified through measures that would require legal support. The prevailing public mood is as Supreme Court Chief Justice John Roberts proclaimed: "The way to stop discrimination on the basis of race is to stop discriminating on the basis of race."[9] When Roberts issued this claim in the Court's majority decision rejecting the idea that there is a "compelling state interest" in pursuing racial integration of public schools, he cited no evidence or argument in support. To this extent, his claim spoke to ideology, not empirical fact or hypothesis. The Roberts Court is now reconsidering *Grutter* and expected to further weaken affirmative action in higher education through the pending ruling in *Fisher v. University of Texas at Austin.*

I proceed from the assumption that not much will be done to promote racial justice through judicial and legislative processes. Rather than adopting the standard civil rights emphasis on legalistic maneuvers and popular moral sentiment, my approach appeals to moral conscience and good faith where they could be expected to make a significant difference.[10] Robust practices of equality of opportunity are especially warranted in response to the historical injustice that continues disproportionately to burden certain social groups. While black Americans are my case study, I am not suggesting that the historical injustice suffered by other social groups is not also relevant or important today.

In the discussion that follows, I argue that mainstream institutions of higher education in the United States have a distinctive moral responsibility to promote racial justice with respect to black Americans. The argument applies to all mainstream institutions of higher education, in various ways, yet anticipates that private institutions will be the main site for corrective race-conscious measures. My working hypothesis is that the legacy of racial injustice is a significant and fundamental source of black socioeconomic disadvantage. Speculation that persons with African ancestry tend to be "naturally" disadvantaged by innate inferiority or that black American cultural dysfunction is an independent source of socioeconomic disadvantage will not be addressed. I will offer proposals for how black progress in education could be advanced through the intervention of colleges and universities—with tacit focus on "elite" institutions, since these are more likely both to have greater resources at their disposal and to offer a more secure path toward socioeconomic gain.[11] Still, these proposals do not exempt nonelite institutions when they have adequate resources and can clear local legal barriers such as state laws prohibiting race-conscious measures.

III

Higher education has not been simply one site, among others, where anti-black racial injustice has occurred. Rather, mainstream institutions of higher education have played a major role in enabling this racialized state of affairs. Well into the twentieth century, historically white colleges and universities applied segregationist norms that discouraged, if not always absolutely prevented, the few qualified blacks there were from enrolling. This is not supposed to be a controversial contention. Historically black colleges and universities (HBCUs) would not have been needed if segregationist norms in mainstream higher education had not been in effect. To acknowledge that the racial caste system necessarily led to underresourced and unequal black institutions is not to disparage the value of HBCUs in providing opportunities for higher education that most qualified black Americans would not have had access to otherwise.

Prior to 1964, when the Civil Rights Act was passed into law, the vast majority of blacks could not take advantage of higher education for obvious reasons. Most were provided basic education of inferior quality. (This has remained the case today, more than fifty years after *Brown v. Board of Education*, in 1954, ruled out de jure racial segregation of public schools.[12]) Opportunities at large for blacks were racially limited. As a long-term proposition, higher education seemed risky and out of reach for average black families in their always more precarious socioeconomic situation. Thus, even if mainstream institutions of higher education had not been racially exclusionary, black Americans still would have been grossly underrepresented there. This does not mean, however, that historically white colleges and universities were not instrumental in helping to perpetuate black disadvantage.

Consider the GI Bill. On its website, the U.S. Department of Veterans Affairs (VA) lauds this bill as "one of the most significant pieces of legislation ever produced by the federal government—one that impacted the United States socially, economically, and politically."[13] A story is then told in greater detail: "Before [World War II], college and homeownership were, for the most part, unreachable dreams for the average American. Thanks to the GI Bill, millions who would have flooded the job market instead opted for education. In the peak year of 1947, veterans accounted for 49 percent of college admissions. By the time the original GI Bill ended on July 25, 1956, 7.8 million of 16 million World War II veterans had participated in an education or training program. . . . Millions also took advantage of the GI Bill's home loan guaranty."[14] The VA does not describe the racial dynamics of the bill's implementation. For that, we have to turn to scholars: "The university came to define and ensure the ongoing production of a white middle class, rather than solely a training ground for the moneyed elite. But because blacks had fewer opportunities to earn college degrees, with or without benefits, the black middle class failed to keep pace. The bill broke down class lines in higher education, but inequities of race remained."[15] Ironically, the VA's web page story about the bill depicts a black male through three life stages— soldier, college graduate, and medical professional—as the representative beneficiary of the program.

In their "balanced history" that "gives us our most comprehensive survey" of the GI Bill's provisions, Glenn Altschuler and Stuart Blumin spin the legislation as a vehicle for positive racial change weighed down by racial prejudice of its time.[16] The bill, they write, "was the most egalitarian and generous initiative blacks had ever experienced. . . . Nonetheless, because the overwhelming majority of beneficiaries were white . . . the GI Bill did not reduce racial disparities in the United States."[17] To translate, this means no net gain for substantive racialized equality. What explains more concretely the racially disparate impact of the legislation during its post–World War II prime? Although the GI Bill formally granted veterans the same benefits on a race-neutral basis, the bill's implementation at the state and local levels was not race neutral. A number of factors dominated circa 1946: segregationist policies enacted by the VA itself; typically weak public schools for blacks that inadequately prepared most of them for college; discriminatory admissions practices at historically white colleges and universities, both southern and northern; overcrowding at HBCUs, limiting the options for many black veterans to vocational training and trade schools (even as fewer apprenticeships were also available to blacks); and generally no access to GI low-interest home mortgage loans.[18]

The economists Sarah Turner and John Bound argue that the GI Bill overall "exacerbated rather than narrowed the economic and educational differences" between blacks and whites.[19] In other words, the bill facilitated a disproportionate distribution of benefits to whites that swamped what benefits blacks received. Turner and Bound's analysis attributes this mostly to racial discrimination in the South, where roughly 80 percent of the black population lived at the end of World War II. The bottom line is that for the vast majority of black veterans, "the educational gains associated with World War II service and the availability of G.I. benefits are consistently indistinguishable from zero."[20] A rising tide lifted millions of whites and far fewer blacks to a secure middle class: the relatively meager gains for blacks as a group—in both education and federally sponsored home ownership, along with commensurate economic advancement—are the data points substantiating the conclusion that blacks fell further behind whites.[21] Unsurprisingly, the GI Bill does not live in lore among black Americans.

There are broader lessons to be drawn from the history of the GI Bill. Turner and Bound suggest that, contrary to the view held by advocates of school choice, who often cite the GI Bill's success as a motivation for vouchers, the bill is an example of how "decentralized federal initiatives" can yield unequal access.[22] This is an interesting and important point to raise about education policy, but I am emphasizing a different lesson about the harm done by racialized inequality. Scholars have underappreciated how bad the GI Bill proved for blacks. Ira Katznelson, for example, concludes:

> It is indisputable that the GI Bill offered eligible African Americans more benefits and more opportunities than they possibly could have imagined in the early 1940s. Yet the way in which the law and its programs were organized and administered, and its ready accommodation to the larger discriminatory context within which it was embedded, produced practices that were more racially distinct and arguably more cruel than any other New Deal–era program. The performance of the GI Bill mocked the promise of fair treatment. The differential treatment meted out to African Americans sharply curtailed the statute's powerful egalitarian promise and significantly widened the country's large racial gap.[23]

This stress on racially unequal treatment buries the lead. The GI Bill made blacks as a group worse off relative to whites.

In gesturing toward a silver lining for blacks, Katznelson is not alone among critics of the GI Bill's implementation. Altschuler and Blumin follow him in characterizing the bill as "de facto affirmative action for whites," yet similarly insist that "the glass was also half full."[24] Turner and Bound observe, "The availability of benefits to Black veterans had a substantial and positive impact on the educational attainment of those [few] likely to have access to colleges and universities outside the South."[25] Hilary Herbold sees wider gains: "Clearly, the GI Bill was a crack in the wall of racism that had surrounded the American university system. It forced predominantly white colleges to allow a larger number of blacks to enroll, contributed to a more diverse curriculum at many HBCUs, and helped provide a foundation for the gradual growth of a black middle class."[26] I am not denying that the GI

Bill yielded various gains for blacks. I am arguing that these gains appear to have amounted to a net loss for blacks, relative to whites, with respect to substantive equality of opportunity—by democratizing, and thereby expanding, material white privilege.

Unfair policy practices are unjust in themselves. But the problem regarding the GI Bill goes deeper than this. Substantive equality of opportunity is compromised by a large racial socioeconomic gap. The GI Bill, by enabling and exacerbating this gap, helped to support white flight from cities and emergent integrated neighborhoods to suburbs segregated through economic effect or, failing that, racially restrictive "covenants."[27] Blacks could be and literally were left behind in underresourced primary and secondary schools—even though the bill, by marginally improving black access to higher education and vocational training, led to economic advancement for blacks relative to their own prior baseline. Higher education was not incidental to a policy through which whites as a group secured greater opportunities in relation to blacks: historically white colleges and universities were, as willing participants, at the center of the GI Bill's practice and its ripple effects.

IV

Mainstream institutions of higher education remain largely complacent actors regarding racial justice. As the case of the GI Bill illustrates, this complacency has long-standing roots in complicity with a racial status quo that was discriminatory in practice when not also in law. By accepting segregationist norms roughly until the civil rights movement compelled changes and then mostly going with the flow of racialized inequality, historically white colleges and universities enabled processes by which whites democratized and consolidated their socioeconomic advantages over blacks. Entrenched racialized inequality in the United States has been made possible in no small part through intergenerational transfers of wealth and opportunity facilitated by education in general and higher education in particular. Far from being hostage to explicitly racist times, mainstream higher education helped to define those times and to secure a legacy of white advantage.

In this light, "complacency" is too charitable a term. Racially exclusionary practices at historically white colleges and universities kept down the numbers of the few blacks who were eligible for admission. This was plainly contrary to the liberal notion of higher education as a means for social progress. There is no reason to think that these institutions—their leaders, faculty, and students—were not well positioned to play a prominent role in challenging discrimination by modeling how a racially just society could look and operate. Their widespread failure to do so is striking. Compare, for instance, President Harry Truman's decision to risk his reelection bid by issuing an executive order in 1948 to integrate the armed forces. The U.S. military went on to become the most racially inclusive mainstream institution in the country.[28] Elite institutions of higher education have since closed the gap at the level of status positions—though this largely reflects stalled progress in the military, apart from the Army. Blacks comprised 5.5 percent (in 2007) of undergraduates at the 146 U.S. colleges and universities rated in the "most" and "highly" selective categories of *Barron's Guide to Colleges*, and 5.3 percent (in 2009) of full-time faculty at U.S. colleges and universities— compared with 12.6 percent (in 2010) of the overall U.S. population.[29]

The transition from racial exclusion to marginal inclusion at historically white colleges and universities also reinforced the message that blacks were not really welcome in de jure integrated society. Outside and inside higher education, there never was a comprehensive plan to integrate blacks fully into American life; that the best, brightest, and most conscientious blacks could expect to be tolerated and to attain a solidly middle-class life did not take the edge off.[30] A version of the message of marginal inclusion seems to endure, especially at selective undergraduate schools and in graduate and professional programs, where blacks continue to be grossly underrepresented as students and faculty at the same time as white resentment of affirmative action has run high.[31] Such a message is hardly blunted, I contend, when the basis of concern about racial inclusivity is shifted from a commitment to racial justice to a more diffuse interest in "diversity." In principle, my view does not seem incredibly controversial: the causal impact of past racial injustice in higher education shapes what justice requires in higher education in the future.

I anticipate the objection that institutions, unlike persons, cannot be bearers of moral responsibility. Racialized mistakes were made at historically white colleges and universities mainly prior to 1964. Persons responsible for the exclusionary practices back then are gone from the active scene. So how can it make sense to hold these institutions today, and the persons now responsible for their practices, morally accountable for the mistakes of actors long past?

This objection misconstrues my argument. The view I am defending does not treat institutions like persons in any literal sense—say, along the lines of the Supreme Court's decision in *Citizens United v. Federal Election Commission* (2010), which recognized for corporations a right of freedom of expression that permits corporate electioneering. Rather, I am appealing only to the causal impact of historical injustice done to blacks through mainstream institutions of higher education. Such institutions have pasts demonstrably connected to the present state of racialized inequality by way of: (1) a general role in expanding white socioeconomic advantage relative to that of blacks, which successive generations of whites have had the opportunity to parlay in the realm of education itself at all levels; and (2) a specific role in giving a vastly disproportionate number of whites the admissions benefit of legacy status at schools from which their family members graduated.[32]

Mainstream institutions of higher education are not analogous to a defunct corporation whose employees had been poorly paid and whose shareholders were wiped out, leaving no discernible and sustained impact other than the physical facilities and the company name acquired by new ownership. My claim is not that moral responsibility for historical injustice itself, like Christianity's doctrine of original sin, is passed on to successive generations of actors in an institution. My claim is that forward-looking moral responsibility to correct an unjust legacy of benefits and burdens can transfer to current actors in an institution. Historically white colleges and universities seem eager to draw connections with their pasts while ignoring or downplaying the racial ramifications. Perhaps the charge of hypocrisy could be avoided by disowning both credit and blame for past deeds. But this represents a radical proposal that, practically speaking, would prompt a major overhaul of admissions and fund-raising approaches and, theoretically speaking, would require a major revision in how sustainable entities—from academic institutions to families to countries—morally regard connections with their pasts. Presumably, no such departures are in the offing. Nor would disowning both credit and blame for the past be morally plausible, namely, when an unjust past remains causally connected to a presently unequal distribution of benefits and burdens.

Another objection I anticipate concerns the limits of compensatory approaches to historical injustice. Some skeptics maintain that individuals eligible for compensation should have to demonstrate specific harms and seek redress from the specific parties, whether individuals or institutions, who either did the harm themselves or directly benefited from it. Other skeptics suggest that there are cases of historical injustice (e.g., slavery and Jim Crow) so profound that duly compensating a broad class of victims (including descendants) is unfeasible. While I am not sympathetic to either version of skepticism about compensatory approaches to historical injustice, I do not need to explore the issue further here. My argument in support of corrective practices in higher education is not about compensation.

The relevant difference between corrective justice and compensatory justice can be summed up as follows. Corrective justice aims to rectify current inequalities that to a significant extent stem from historical injustice. If the class of persons harmed by historical injustice is no longer suffering the effects of that harm—measured against standard indicators of socioeconomic equality within a society—then the requirement of corrective justice would not be triggered. By contrast, compensatory justice aims to compensate victims for their losses, period, regardless of how well or poorly the victims (including descendants) are doing at some later time. I am arguing that in the context of higher education in the United States, the requirement of corrective justice is triggered in the case of black Americans. Whether blacks are also due straight compensation for the historical injustice they have suffered is a more contentious question that is beyond the scope of the argument I have made.

V

There is no denying that the racial situation at mainstream institutions of higher education has changed for the better.[33] Although discrimination at historically white colleges and universities was a norm prior to 1964, the mantra of diversity is a norm today. Black students "well qualified" for admission are now encouraged to apply. Most selective private colleges and universities practice some form of race-conscious affirmative action. The question, then, is whether the abandonment of overtly exclusionary racial practices and the addition of inclusionary measures at the point of entry are sufficient for mainstream higher education to fulfill its responsibility to promote corrective racial justice.

The answer is no. A diversity rationale for affirmative action does not make the appropriate connections between the policy, the racially unjust past, and ongoing racialized inequality. To describe black Americans simply as a "historically underrepresented" group in higher education is euphemistic and misleading, as if the reasons so few blacks attended mainstream institutions were entirely beyond the institutions' control. Emphasis on a diversity rationale allows historically white colleges and universities to evade acknowledging and taking ownership of their role in perpetuating racial injustice—which had direct effects on individuals and group-level effects that have helped to sustain white advantage and black disadvantage.

In a spirit similar to my argument, Supreme Court Justice Ruth Bader Ginsburg has expressed dissatisfaction with a diversity rationale for affirmative action. "If we take seriously the promises of employment, education, and sustenance made in the Universal Declaration of Human Rights," she argues, "the discrepancies in racial well-being in the United States noted by the [1995] United Nations report demand affirmative government action."[34] Ginsburg went on to advance this view in her concurring opinion in *Grutter* and her dissenting opinion in *Gratz*. Citing the International Convention on the Elimination of All Forms of Racial Discrimination (CERD) and the Convention on the Elimination of All Forms of Discrimination against Women (CEDAW), her *Gratz* opinion states, "'The Constitution is color conscious to prevent discrimination being perpetuated and to undo the effects of past discrimination.' . . . . Contemporary human rights documents draw just this line; they distinguish between policies of oppression and measures designed to accelerate *de facto* equality."[35] International law and commonsense application of the U.S. Constitution (viz., unjust harms that still have major effects warrant real remedies) are on Ginsburg's side.

Diversity, whatever its benefits apart from corrective justice, is an incomplete rationale for corrective policies such as affirmative action for black Americans. To separate such policies from a corrective-justice basis is to expose them to criticism that they violate standards of fairness. By contrast, a corrective-justice basis for race-conscious policies is not nearly as susceptible to moral complaint about departures from public ideals of color blindness and individual meritocracy. My assumption is that a large white-black socioeconomic gap in the United States is to a significant extent a result of historical injustice. Otherwise, the explanation would have to be that blacks somehow are endogenously disadvantaged to a degree that roughly corresponds to the extent of the gap—that blacks themselves are mainly to blame. An explanation of this sort seems to me untenable.

Focus on the legacy of historical injustice as the rationale for corrective racial justice practices would specify and widen the imperative for action. According to the *Journal of Blacks in Higher Education*, "Many black students come from families that have no tradition of higher education. There can be a lack of necessary support and understanding for nurturing the black student's effort to succeed in higher education."[36] But money, or rather a lack of it, appears to be the primary factor for the low college graduation rate (about 45 percent) of black students: an estimated two-thirds of black students who drop out of college do so for financial reasons.[37] The lack of money among black students can be attributed to the lack of wealth in black families—which can be tied to a history of racial subordination that includes strongly white-biased policies such as the original GI Bill. In short, mainstream institutions of higher education in the United States are deeply implicated in the history and legacy of antiblack racial injustice. This is the basis of the distinctive moral responsibility these institutions have to be concerned about substantive equality of opportunity with respect to blacks in particular.

The moral inadequacy of diversity as a rationale for affirmative action might help to explain the practical inadequacy of affirmative action as a means for addressing black underrepresentation in higher education. When increasing the number of successful black students in higher education is a goal, discussion is steered away from the question of whether affirmative action is unfair because the practice burdens meritorious nonblack individuals for the sake of benefiting less meritorious blacks. Instead, the standard practice of affirmative action would appear to be unfair because it does not contribute enough toward a remedy for black socioeconomic disadvantage enabled by higher education over generations. The basic argument for this claim is uncomplicated: selective colleges and universities are competing amongst themselves for a small pool of qualified black students, not (directly) expanding the pool of qualified black students. For instance, if Harvard University had much less of a commitment to affirmative action, those black students who probably would not otherwise get into Harvard would still be strong enough to get into very good, albeit less competitive or prestigious, schools without the benefit of affirmative action.

My point is not that most black beneficiaries of affirmative action at selective colleges and universities tend to be undeserving of an unnecessary benefit since they, like other high-achieving students in the United States, disproportionately come from middle-class backgrounds and would do reasonably well without the benefit. It is a mistake to suppose that black students whose families are not generally underprivileged are not burdened as members of a racially stigmatized group—and thus are not due any (direct) benefit from corrective-justice policies. But if affirmative action ultimately has the goal of changing the group dynamics of black disadvantage, as attempting to correct the legacy of historical injustice would involve, the standard practice seems insufficiently inclusive.

To be clear, I am not suggesting an argument against affirmative action in higher education. Corrective-justice aims are advanced—for example, by countering stereotypes and stereotype threat—when more black Americans succeed in challenging and prestigious academic environments. Without affirmative action, even fewer blacks would be in that position. As the famous study by William Bowen and Derek Bok found, substituting class-conscious for race-conscious policies will not deliver comparable results.[38] (This finding confirms common sense: in a society long marked by racial subordination, in which blacks make up about 13 percent of the population, we can expect far fewer black students from nonprivileged backgrounds who are as qualified, by the conventional measures of grades and test scores, as their white counterparts.) I am suggesting that as applied to black Americans, the standard practice of affirmative action has been an easy way to benefit members of a social group burdened by historical injustice without doing enough to benefit the group overall. There is an element of bad faith in this practice, which makes a show of conscience: popular and political resistance to race-conscious policies lends the impression that a modest effort, under the morally vague cover of diversity, is probably the most that can be hoped for.

The argument that mainstream higher education has failed to satisfy its responsibility of corrective justice toward black Americans calls for constructive proposals. Colleges and universities, through realistic measures, could do significantly better. At the point of entry, this would require greater support, academically and financially, for black students in the realm to be admitted. The deeper difference would come prior to the point of entry, where this would not rely on waiting for wholesale improvements downstream to produce more of those students. In closing, I sketch a proposal for the latter possibility.

VI

Mainstream institutions of higher education, as a standard part of their practice, could sponsor academy schools geared to serving underprivileged black students at the primary and secondary levels. Instead of typically doing nothing systemic to improve the quality of black students downstream and then competing for the few qualified ones available at admissions time, colleges and universities could take an active role in producing future black students qualified for higher education. Examples of such academy-type schools already exist, prominent among them the University of California, San Diego's Preuss School (grades 6–12) and the University of Chicago Charter School (grades prekindergarten-12).[39] Preuss and UChicago Charter serve underprivileged children in areas that have large minority populations, without explicitly targeting particular racial or ethnic groups (which sidesteps color-blind politics). So there is reason to believe that colleges and universities, public and private, can undertake promising interventions downstream on behalf of children in need. This claim about institutional feasibility does not depend on accepting the corrective-justice-based focus on black students that I have defended. As UChicago Charter demonstrates, though, an ostensibly race-neutral rationale and practice can have a disparate impact on black students when such schools are located in black neighborhoods.

An academy schools approach, as I conceive of it, is roughly analogous to the model for producing professional soccer players in Europe and South America through academy programs sponsored by major clubs (e.g., FC Barcelona in Spain, Manchester United FC in England, and Santos FC in Brazil). These clubs are not merely hoping to sign prospects at the age of seventeen or eighteen; signing and development start as early as age twelve. Soccer clubs "growing their own" future players is not, of course, a matter of justice: the soccer academy model is driven by competitive and economic self-interest. But the disanalogy in motivations between higher education and professional sports does not indicate a damaging disanalogy in efficacy. An academy approach would have greater efficacy for education, since there will be a much better rate of success developing young people for college (or other kinds of postsecondary learning) than for the rarefied domain of professional sports. Institutions of higher education could be expected to provide financial resources, sustained commitment, and broad oversight—not hands-on administration and teaching that would require expertise they typically lack at the primary and secondary levels.

My academy schools proposal does not represent a general endorsement of charter schools over public schools. I am sympathetic to Diane Ravitch's criticisms of the "school reform" agenda, with its overwhelming focus on governance and standards. Her guarded praise of the Harlem Children's Zone charter schools, for instance, mostly attributes their success to greater resources—academic, social, and medical, heavily funded by corporations and philanthropists—and not better instruction, in comparison to nearby public schools.[40] This assessment is plausible, as is Ravitch's emphasis on improving instruction through means known to make a difference. Further, there is scant evidence that teachers' unions or bad teachers are at the root of the problem of black educational disadvantage.[41]

That said, my academy schools proposal does accept a selective dimension, which is in tension with the ideal of public schools as a source of equal opportunity. High-commitment schools, as they have been called, are charter schools that serve underprivileged neighborhoods and feature "longer school days, stringent disciplinary norms, and rigorous 'basics' academic curriculums."[42] The selective dimension of these schools typically includes two features: they choose their students through a lottery parents must apply for, and they choose students who have demonstrated academic talent. Children with disengaged parents will be excluded by default from the lottery process. This constitutes a double disadvantage: not only are such children already burdened by having disengaged parents, they also are subsequently burdened by not being candidates for a more productive learning environment. I acknowledge that the resources and selection issues, and not better instruction, are probably the main factors contributing to a learning environment that is more productive in high-commitment schools as compared to nearby public schools. From an ideal perspective, the added disadvantage of a parental-action lottery is unfair to children with disengaged parents.

The official rejoinder is that high-commitment schools would like to figure out how to expand the applicant pool to include the disengaged population. Yet this seems doubtful as a full explanation. Why couldn't students, or academically eligible students, automatically be entered into application lotteries, without the need for prior parental action? One reason for not employing this procedure is that high-commitment schools depend on parental engagement in support of the more demanding academic and disciplinary expectations these schools have: the lottery selection effect is a significant factor in the relative success of these schools and their students. To put the point more bluntly: parental engagement contributes to and is thereby a predictor of a child's educational success, so the default exclusion of children with disengaged parents helps to benefit the more promising segment of the underprivileged student population.[43] Since there is nothing mysterious or unforeseeable about this selection effect, which could easily enough be avoided, we can assume that it often is a wanted (if not exactly intended) result—limiting access to and making more efficient use of scarce, education-oriented resources and opportunities.

Proper justice does not permit a wealthy society to starve itself of the public resources necessary to provide substantive equality of opportunity, especially for the most disadvantaged and vulnerable. But I am addressing the issue of what is to be done given actual conditions that predictably will fall far short of proper justice—namely, with regard to black progress under circumstances of socioeconomic crisis and inadequate political action. The problems weighing on underprivileged black communities are so dire and complex, and the promise of comprehensive change so remote, that I am openly defending a triage approach in education. This approach endorses an alternative path for underprivileged black children who—by virtue of whatever combination of parental engagement, academic talent, and life ambition—are already in a better position to contribute to and take advantage of a more productive learning environment than that in their regular schools. Their less fortunate peers would be left to "unsorted" regular schools and the more distant hope of significantly better educational outcomes there.

Academy schools need not be exclusionary on the basis of parental engagement or academic talent. College and universities, without these exclusions, still could helpfully intervene downstream: the infusion of resources from outside primary and secondary public school systems can be separated from the selective dimension in choosing which underprivileged students to develop through an alternative path. On grounds of urgency and efficiency, however, I am proposing a triage approach as morally legitimate and compelling under severely nonideal conditions. I am not, in contrast to reform advocates fixated on "school choice,"[44] looking to charter schools of any type as a key to eliminating educational disadvantage. Indeed, the resources and selection issues that largely seem to explain why high-commitment schools are relatively successful also would explain why such schools could not be scaled up as the major feature of a solution.[45]

A triage approach in education has the purpose of saving as many underprivileged black children from bad school environments as limited resources and opportunities, apart from those normally required by law, would enable. This does yield the following consequences, outlined by Harry Brighouse and Gina Schouten:

> Students whose parents do not enter the lottery—students who are liable to be among the very most disconnected and disadvantaged—are concentrated in regular schools. The more concentrated the presence of high-commitment schools in a region, the higher will be the concentration of extreme disadvantage in the regular schools in that region. There is evidence, furthermore, of peer effects on student learning: that learning in a classroom with harder-working, higher-achieving, and less disruptive peers increases a student's own learning; the converse is that less-hardworking, lower-achieving, and more disruptive peers harms a student's own learning. . . . If so, then some if not all of the amelioration of educational disadvantage that high-commitment schools generate may be gained at the cost of increasing the educational disadvantage of those students who concentrate in the regular nonchoice schools.[46]

These considerations should not be taken lightly. Nevertheless, black children in low-performing schools seem to be doing so badly as a group that any loss to the lower-achieving students in positive peer effects might well occur below a threshold at which there would be much difference to educational outcomes among that lower-achieving subset, as measured by subsequent academic qualification for college. Reality suggests that the current state of black educational disadvantage is generally such that higher-achieving underprivileged students are critically burdened by being hostage to their regular schools, while lower-achieving students are not critically benefited by the presence of their higher-achieving peers in those schools.

My academy schools proposal, especially a triage version, would provide a far more likely path to higher education for a substantially greater number of underprivileged black children. Triage is never a solution to a crisis: the goal in this case, as always, is to make a crisis less severe.

I have argued that mainstream institutions of higher education bear a distinctive responsibility to deal seriously with black disadvantage in education at all levels. While my argument might be controversial in various respects, its central aim is to prompt hard thinking about black progress under nonideal conditions.

Notes

I would like to thank Jaime Ahlberg, Harry Brighouse, Diana Hess, Erin Kelly, and Michael McPherson for comments; Paula Frederick for research assistance; and the Spencer Foundation for a grant supporting this research.

1. While studies may differ in how to measure a liberal orientation, study data indicate that the academic community in the United States is more liberal than the overall population, if less so than often supposed. See, e.g., Amy Liu, Sylvia Ruiz, Linda DeAngelo, and John Pryor, *Findings from the 2008 Administration of the College Senior Survey (CSS): National Aggregates* (Los Angeles: Higher Education Research Institute, UCLA, 2009), 29–30; and Patricia Cohen, "Professors' Liberalism Contagious? Maybe Not," *New York Times*, November 2, 2008.
2. See, e.g., John Rawls, *A Theory of Justice*, rev. ed. (Cambridge, MA: Harvard University Press, 1999).
3. See, e.g., Charles W. Mills, "Retrieving Rawls for Racial Justice? A Critique of Tommie Shelby," *Critical Philosophy of Race* 1 (2013): 1–27.
4. Richard Arneson, for example, supports a "prioritarian doctrine" of "egalitarian welfarism," which expresses no particular concern for corrective justice in the provision and distribution of higher education. Fairness would require prioritizing gains in quality of life for persons who are worse off—regardless of the justice circumstances that may have contributed to disadvantage. In the case of education, the egalitarian welfarist would focus on "policies that improve the pre-school, elementary school, and secondary school learning of those children whose parents lack college education and those whose parents are low-income." See Richard J. Arneson, "Justice in Access to Higher Education," unpublished manuscript, University of California, San Diego.
5. See, e.g., William G. Bowen and Derek Bok, *The Shape of the River: Long-Term Consequences of Considering Race in College and University Admissions* (Princeton, NJ: Princeton University Press, 2000).
6. *Grutter v. Bollinger*, 539 U.S. 306, 343 (2003).
7. Peter Schmidt, "Sandra Day O'Connor Revisits and Revives Affirmative-Action Controversy," *Chronicle of Higher Education*, January 14, 2010. Cited from the original in Sandra Day O'Connor and Stewart J. Schwab, "Twenty-five Years: A Need for Study and Action," in *The Next Twenty-five Years: Affirmative Action in Higher Education in the United States and South Africa*, ed. David L. Featherman, Martin Hall, and Marvin Krislov (Ann Arbor: University of Michigan Press, 2010).

8. See, e.g., Elizabeth Anderson, *The Imperative of Integration* (Princeton, NJ: Princeton University Press, 2010); Dalton Conley, *Being Black, Living in the Red: Race, Wealth, and Social Policy in America* (Berkeley and Los Angeles: University of California Press, 1999); and Thomas M. Shapiro, *The Hidden Cost of Being African American: How Wealth Perpetuates Inequality* (New York: Oxford University Press, 2004).

9. *Parents Involved in Community Schools v. Seattle School District No. 1*, 551 U.S. 701 (2007).

10. In a similar spirit, see Jack Turner, *Awakening to Race: Individualism and Social Consciousness in America* (Chicago: University of Chicago Press, 2012). Turner defends a version of American "individualism" that instead of being postracial would be expressed through joining in a public commitment to fighting racial injustice.

11. For concerns about whether a college degree generally remains a good investment, see, e.g., "Not What It Used to Be: American Universities Represent Declining Value for Money to Their Students," *Economist*, December 1, 2012.

12. See, e.g., Jonathan Kozol, *The Shame of the Nation: The Restoration of Apartheid Schooling in America* (New York: Crown, 2005).

13. U.S. Department of Veteran Affairs, http://gibill.va.gov/benefits/history_timeline/index.html.

14. Ibid.

15. Hilary Herbold, "Never a Level Playing Field: Blacks and the GI Bill," *Journal of Blacks in Higher Education* 6 (1994–95): 106.

16. Glenn C. Altschuler and Stuart M. Blumin, *The GI Bill: A New Deal for Veterans* (New York: Oxford University Press, 2009), ix.

17. Ibid., 129.

18. Herbold, "Never a Level Playing Field," 106–7. Roughly the same factors are also described in Altschuler and Blumin, *The GI Bill*.

19. Sarah E. Turner and John Bound, "Closing the Gap or Widening the Divide: The Effects of the G.I. Bill and World War II on the Educational Outcomes of Black Americans," *Journal of Economic History* 63 (2003): 145–77; cited from NBER Working Paper 9044, 24–25.

20. Ibid., 19. My interpretation is consistent with Turner and Bound's finding that (the much smaller proportion of) blacks from outside the South made significant gains compared to blacks from southern states.

21. On the relation between home ownership and the disparity between blacks and whites in average family net worth, see, e.g., Shapiro, *The Hidden Cost of Being African American*, 107–9. Also see Melvin L. Oliver and Thomas M. Shapiro, *Black Wealth/White Wealth: A New Perspective on Racial Inequality* (New York: Routledge, 1995).

22. Turner and Bound, "Closing the Gap or Widening the Divide," 24.

23. Ira Katznelson, *When Affirmative Was White: An Untold History of Racial Inequality in Twentieth-Century America* (New York: Norton, 2005), 140–41.

24. Altschuler and Blumin, *The GI Bill*, 136.

25. Turner and Bound, "Closing the Gap or Widening the Divide"; cited from NBER Working Paper 9044, 25.

26. Herbold, "Never a Level Playing Field," 108.

27. See, e.g., the discussion of VA and FHA (Federal Housing Administration) segregationist policy in Altschuler and Blumin, *The GI Bill*, 198–203.

28. One measure for comparing racial inclusivity is the degree to which blacks hold status positions. See, e.g., Charles Moskos, "Mandating Inclusion: The Military as a Social Lab," *Current* 354 (1993): 20–26; and Ronald Roach, "Doing What Had to Be

Done: The Integrated Military Seen as Model for Society," *Black Issues in Higher Education* 14 (1997): 18–19.

29. Blacks comprised 11–12 percent (in 2008) of Army officers—compared with 4–8 percent of officers in the Navy, Air Force, and Marines. See Mike Mills, "Five Years Post-Grutter, Little Progress in Black and Latino/a Enrollments at Selective Colleges and Universities," *Journal of College Admission* (2010): 6–7; "Black Faculty at the Nation's Highest-Ranked Universities," *Journal of Blacks in Higher Education Weekly Bulletin*, October 22, 2009, http://www.jbhe.com/latest/index102209.html; U.S. Census Bureau, http://quickfacts.census.gov/qfd/states/00000.html; and Lolita C. Baldor, "After 60 Years, Black Officers Rare," Associated Press, July 23, 2008.

30. See, e.g., Ellis Cose, *The Rage of a Privileged Class: Why Are Middle-Class Blacks Angry? Why Should America Care?* (New York: HarperCollins, 1993).

31. Data drawn from national samples in the early and mid-1990s showed that "while over 70 percent of Euro-Americans asserted that other Euro-Americans were likely being hurt by affirmative action for Afro-Americans, only 7 percent claimed to have actually experienced any form of reverse discrimination and only 16 percent knew of someone close who had." See Orlando Patterson, *The Ordeal of Integration: Progress and Resentment in America's "Racial" Crisis* (Washington, DC: Civitas Counterpoint, 1997), 148. Also see, e.g., Lawrence Bobo, "Race and Beliefs about Affirmative Action: Assessing the Effects of Interests, Group Threat, Ideology, and Racism," in *Racialized Politics: The Debate about Racism in America*, ed. David O. Sears, Jim Sidanius, and Lawrence Bobo (Chicago: University of Chicago Press, 2000).

32. See, e.g., Daniel Golden, *The Price of Admission: How America's Ruling Class Buys Its Way into Elite Colleges—And Who Gets Left Outside the Gates* (New York: Crown, 2006). According to Golden, alumni children at Notre Dame, for instance, were the largest group receiving preferential admission circa 2003: nearly one in four students was an alumni child, while 4 percent were African American and 8 percent were Hispanic.

33. Data collected on aggregate college enrollments show an increase of 12 percent for blacks aged eighteen to twenty-four from 1980 (19.7) to 2008 (32.1). See Susan Aud, Mary Ann Fox, and Angelina KewalRamani, *Status and Trends in the Education of Racial and Ethnic Minorities* (NCES 2010–015), U.S. Department of Education, National Center for Education Statistics (Washington, DC: Government Printing Office, 2010), http://nces.ed.gov/pubs2010/2010015.pdf.

34. Ruth Bader Ginsburg, "Affirmative Action as an International Human Rights Dialogue: Considered Opinion," Brookings Institution, Winter 2000, http://www.brookings.edu/articles/2000/winter_politics_ginsburg.aspx.

35. *Gratz v. Bollinger*, 539 U.S. 244, 302 (2003).

36. "College Graduation Rates: Where Black Students Do the Best and Where They Fare Poorly Compared to Their White Peers," *Journal of Blacks in Higher Education* (Autumn 2009), http://www.jbhe.com/features/65_gradrates.html.

37. Ibid.

38. See Bowen and Bok, "The Admissions Process and 'Race-Neutrality,'" in *The Shape of the River*.

39. See http://preuss.ucsd.edu/ and http://uei-schools.org/uccs/site/default.asp. The UCSD Preuss School lists its student demographics as "67% Hispanic, 11% African American, 19% Asian/Indo-Chinese and 3% Caucasian/Other," while the University of Chicago Charter School serves a predominantly black population based on Chicago public schools attendance boundaries.

40. See Diane Ravitch, "The Myth of Charter Schools," *New York Review of Books*, Novem-

ber 11, 2010. Also see Diane Ravitch, *The Death and Life of the Great American School System: How Testing and Choice Are Undermining Education* (New York: Basic Books, 2010).

41. I lean toward an "external-to-schools" account of the root causes of black educational disadvantage—which is compatible with seeking "internal-to-schools" improvement. See, e.g., Richard Rothstein, *Class and Schools: Using Social, Economic, and Educational Reform to Close the Black-White Achievement Gap* (Washington, DC: Economic Policy Institute, 2004).

42. Harry Brighouse and Gina Schouten, "Understanding the Context for Existing Reform and Research Proposals," in *Whither Opportunity? Rising Inequality, Schools, and Children's Life Chances*, ed. Greg J. Duncan and Richard J. Murnane (New York: Russell Sage Foundation, 2011), 507.

43. I owe my elaboration of this point to comments from Harry Brighouse.

44. See, e.g., Abigail Thernstrom and Stephan Thernstrom, *No Excuses: Closing the Racial Gap in Learning* (New York: Simon & Schuster, 2003).

45. For a detailed argument along these lines, see Brighouse and Schouten, "Understanding the Context for Existing Reform and Research Proposals," 517–18.

46. Ibid., 519. These consequences would apply not just to high-commitment schools but to any program providing exit options for children from underprivileged neighborhoods. For instance, the Metco Program in Massachusetts is "a voluntary program intended to expand educational opportunities, increase diversity, and reduce racial isolation by permitting [racial-minority] students in certain cities to attend public schools in other [predominantly white, suburban] communities that have agreed to participate"; http://www.doe.mass.edu/metco/.

EIGHT

Modeling Justice in Higher Education

ERIN I. KELLY

I

Some scholars argue that a liberal arts education fosters critical thinking and promotes democratic values. I argue that a liberal arts education indeed has this potential but that institutional limitations inhibit its fuller development. Meeting certain institutional requirements of justice—including fair equality of opportunity—is critical to the functioning of colleges and universities as just institutions that support critical and creative thinking, ethical reasoning, and democratic ideals. This argues for revising certain popular conceptions of value and merit in college admissions and in academic scholarship, and for developing a campus environment that will enable all students to engage in critical, creative, and ethical thinking within and beyond the university.

II

The United States has had a strong history of liberal arts orientation in education that stresses breadth of intellectual exposure to the humanities, arts, social sciences, mathematics, and natural sciences in a learning environment characterized by Socratic inquiry, reflection, dialogue, and essay writing. The concept of liberal arts education is, broadly speaking, education to allow the flourishing of individuals and society at large. Liberal arts education aims to equip individuals with the knowledge, critical-thinking skills, experience, and capacity for reflection that will enable them to lead thoughtful, fulfilling lives as individuals and to participate cooperatively and productively in politics, the economy, and other spheres of social life. This was the vision of Horace Mann, William James, John Dewey, W. E. B. Du Bois, and other great educators in American history. They were, to be sure, influenced by Plato and

Jean-Jacques Rousseau and also by well-established examples of university systems in Europe, especially England. Still, a liberal arts model seems to have evolved in broader form in the United States, penetrating secondary schools to some extent, as well as being thoroughly established in many American universities and colleges and emphasizing, more than in Europe, a participatory, democratic ideal.

In emphasizing liberal arts education as a means to collective as well as individual flourishing, defenders of liberal arts education stress its value as good preparation for democratic citizenship. They claim that by challenging students to consider a variety of perspectives, experiences, and values, liberal arts education develops the imagination, a capacity for empathy and understanding, and a reflective appreciation of value pluralism.[1] This development might happen in the imaginative engagement with characters in a work of literature, by considering a philosopher's reflections and skeptical questions, through comparative study of different historical eras and cultures, by grasping the dynamics of social groups, by identifying the empirical causes of social change, and so forth. The various disciplinary approaches all require students to consider a subject from a vantage point that is not merely subjective and to make judgments of relevance in relation to parameters that are significant to some or many human beings even though they might not reflect the student's own values. It is argued, and I think reasonably so, that developing these skills helps to enable people in a diverse society and world better to understand one another and to work together.

Advocates also claim that because liberal arts education emphasizes learning and the accumulation of knowledge as a collective endeavor that depends on active participation and codeliberation, it cultivates a democratic culture of inclusion. When conclusions must be based on evidence that can be evaluated by other people and are supported by rational argument rather than mere appeals to authority, participants in intellectual inquiry can reckon with each other as equals.[2] Rational discussion involves taking one's interlocutor seriously as a person with a capacity for rational thought, inquiry, and judgment. These qualities mark persons as equals in a relevant political sense—as fit to participate fully in political society and to enjoy all the rights and benefits of citizenship. Affirming through rational dialogue the status of participants as political equals is an important source of support for democratic institutions. Furthermore, reckoning with the equal standing in conversation of one's interlocutors helps participants to develop the virtues of reasonableness and mutual respect, despite disagreements that arise between them.[3] These virtues are valuable to the democratic process.

Proponents of liberal arts education emphasize that in these ways aspects of intellectual, emotional, and social development promoted through liberal arts education are important to the healthy functioning of a democratic polity. These are important points, and we should be concerned about overly narrow assessments of educational outcomes. In particular, we should be wary of a quantitative, market-oriented "knowledge and skills" model that neglects assessments of innovative, reflective, creative, and collective thinking.[4] In an era of standardized testing and demands on students to memorize and regurgitate volumes of information, we must retain broad and balanced indicators of social health in educational outcomes. Higher education contributes to socially valuable outcomes in ways that standardized testing and statistical measurements of income earning potential are likely to miss.[5] The contribution of liberal arts education to creativity and critical thinking, for example, might well be crucial for research and innovation across a broad spectrum of fields of learning as well as for the development of leadership, cooperation, and problem-solving skills.

Still, we should not oversell the contribution of liberal arts education to the realization of a broader democratic and egalitarian political culture. The goal of generating an inclusive, liberal, intellectually rich and informed political culture in American society is beyond the power of universities alone to achieve.[6] Obstacles to achieving a just democratic society are significant and dispersed throughout our society. They include glaring and consequential socioeconomic inequalities and also institutionally and sociologically entrenched forms of race and gender bias. Broad social change would be required to transform this.

Neither should we uncritically endorse and defend the status quo of liberal arts education itself. The primary beneficiaries of rational dialogue between equals are the people who participate, and their experience is conditioned by the nature of the deliberative community. While our universities and colleges are more inclusive than they once were, they are characterized by many of the same unjust inequalities that characterize other civic realms. This limits the value of liberal arts education as preparation for democratic citizenship. Colleges and universities are in a good position to address this problem. The institutions of higher education could work more effectively to rectify unjust inequalities restricting access to higher education and the community of scholarship. This is especially urgent in elite institutions that are selective. Pursuit of the goal of greater inclusion could help to advance justice within the university. By achieving more inclusive representation by race, gender, and socioeconomic status, institutions of higher education, and liberal arts institutions, in particular, could also serve as models of justice for other institutions. While this would not directly effect change beyond the university, it could, by example, publicly raise the bar for the evaluation of other institutions. By shaping the experience of its members in ethically desirable ways, an inclusive learning community is also potentially self-transformative. A model of education as the collective undertaking of an inclusive and deliberative community of equals has never been fully realized on a scale as large as that of a college or university.[7] Yet it is the best model we have of justice and self-realization. Achieving more inclusive representation is our best hope for increasing the potential of institutions of higher learning to make a positive contribution to broader social justice.

Thus, while it is doubtful that colleges and universities could effectively transform American society into one that is genuinely democratic, they could do something more modest: they could model justice. They could strive to be just communities. This essay explores the virtues of a model of higher education as an inclusive, deliberative, and collective enterprise with potential agency for beneficial and broader social change.

III

Modeling justice in institutions of higher education through fair inclusion by race, gender, and socioeconomic status would require revising some other familiar and relevant models of the value and function of the university:

1. The first is an *economic development model* of the university as an instrument for advancing society's economic growth. In this model, educational outcomes are assessed by their contribution to aggregate economic growth. Contribution to economic growth, regionally and nationally, is of course a familiar aspect of the mission of many schools. For example, a 2003 report commissioned by the eight research universities in the Boston area claims that those universities "not only have a large direct financial impact, but more importantly, they form much of the intellectual underpinning of the regional economy, producing human capital and new technologies that fuel economic growth."[8] The eight presidents of those universities signed the report with evident pride and approval.

    By emphasizing economic development as a model, I refer to the view that the contribution of higher education to national economic growth is its primary justification. Universities themselves do not commonly adopt this model but are sometimes pressured to justify their public funding by at least implicit appeals to this view. A problem with the economic development model is that its aggregative approach neglects matters of the distribution of wealth in society. Furthermore, this model lacks an ethical evaluation of the goals and effects of investment and spending. Without a conception of distributive justice or an ethics of investment and consumption, the economic model is an impoverished perspective from which to evaluate the aims of higher education.[9]

2. The second is a *business model* of the university as offering services demanded by its paying customers. According to this model, a university education should benefit students in line with their expressed aims and goals, such as career advancement, competitive advantage, and increased social status. This model is misguided but not lightly dismissed. Higher education should serve important interests of students, but its aim is not restricted to this mission. A business model of higher education is too individualistic and uncritical. It lacks a collective, public dimension expressing shareable evaluative criteria and joint aims.[10] Just institutions do not merely serve people's existing aims, goals, and self-identified needs; they shape and limit valued aims in line with fair consideration of the interests of all members and, more broadly, of stakeholders. This is an abstract way of saying that universities should guide their members in formulating personal aims and interests that are in line with a broader conception of the social good and the university's role in public life. Since institutions of higher education confer upon their graduates the goods of social status and a competitive advantage in seeking employment, they should do this responsibly: with sensitivity to whether conferring these advantages selectively could be justified to those who lack them.

3. The third is a *scholarcentric model* of the university as a platform for scholarly research with disciplinary autonomy. This model is attractive to research faculty. What I most challenge here is not the value of excellence in research but the value of disciplinary autonomy in the design of departments to suit the research agendas and disciplinary commitments of current faculty.[11] Thus I do not reject a scholarcentric model of the university, but I would qualify it. A paradigm of disciplinary autonomy is not sensitive enough to whether the quest for knowledge advances the ethical value of knowledge. Modeling social justice must include examining the ethical value of scholarly pursuits. This means that those pursuits should be open to meaningful evaluation and criticism by members of the broader university community who are charged with promoting greater inclusiveness, whether university committees, external reviewers, or those in positions of academic leadership perform this assessment.

Criticizing a scholarcentric model of the university is controversial among research faculty and is in tension with some rationales for the tenure system. The tension arises because these measures challenge the autonomy of scholars to define what is of value within their fields, which is what the tenure system protects. I do not advocate eliminating the tenure system, which I think is important for other reasons. But I do support revising the ideal of the university as a platform for scholarly research with disciplinary autonomy, despite the tension this brings with the rationale for tenure. Revisions of a scholarcentric model and the other two prominent and popular conceptions of the social function of the university are needed because of the requirements of social justice for more inclusive representation.

Modeling justice in the university would not displace the other three roles I have described, but it would constrain and balance them so that they contribute to the university's mission without distorting it. Justice is a virtue of the whole institution, organizing and prioritizing its many dimensions.

IV

One might worry about whether it makes sense to model a university after a just society, as justice looks different in different contexts. Plato sought to describe a just soul in order to understand a just city, but a just person might not be like a just city. Perhaps justice is not a uniform value, ordered by similar principles in all of its domains.

In significant ways, just universities are unlike democratic political societies. For example, university presidents are typically chosen not by a democratic vote on campus, but by a university's board of trustees. There are many important differences between a voluntary organization and a political society. Still, we should not thus conclude that the concept of justice is inapplicable to universities. Furthermore, the university as a model of justice is not merely an analogy.

Fair opportunity for education is an entitlement in a just democratic society. I will take this for granted, but it is not exactly clear what this means and how it applies to higher education. For example, should everyone have an opportunity for college education, or are just entitlements to education satisfied by adequate secondary school education? A decent secondary school education might prepare people to participate in civic life, to acquire employment, and to understand the rights and obligations of citizenship. College education is costly, and if that cost is to be shared collectively, its value needs a convincing public justification. Hopeful proclamations about the value of higher education to the further democratization of American political culture do not suffice. On the other hand, a personal-fulfillment rationale for universal college education is also unlikely to survive scrutiny in a pluralistic society.

A compelling basis for staking a fair-opportunity requirement is the actual social function of universities in regulating the production and distribution of wealth, opportunity, and other social goods, such as knowledge, innovation, and culture. The institutions of higher education are major contributors to the preparation of adults for skilled employment, research and development, creative design (in television, film, advertising, and architecture, for example), social commentary and opinion making, and positions of leadership. A college degree is virtually a prerequisite for the promise of recognized social contributions in these arenas. This is a strong reason to maintain that a fair-opportunity requirement extends to institutions of higher learning.[12]

Elite colleges and universities should be subjected to a high level of scrutiny on this measure. Elite institutions have a greater impact on the production and distribution of wealth, opportunity, knowledge, innovation, and culture; admission is highly selective. Furthermore, they are expensive. Students at elite liberal arts institutions spend four years living and studying together, full-time, in an interactive and intensive learning environment. Their peers are not primarily competitors for scarce resources, but partners in a collaborative campus community. This is a resource-intensive endeavor. Careful thinking is required to understand what could make the opportunity to attend fair.

Merit currently plays a role in admissions decisions and is influenced in significant measure by talent, although, as we will see, by other factors as well. If merit is an appropriate criterion, then all potential candidates should have a fair opportunity to be evaluated on their merits. Supposing that fair opportunity is an entitlement and hence should have broad social support, some who share the cost of educating the meritorious would not themselves meet the selection criteria. If this is not unfair, it could only be because there is a rationale for selection by merit that could also be addressed to those who are not selected.

The nature of this rationale, as well as the content of merit judgments itself, will be a function of an understanding of the proper social function of the university; this, in turn, connects with questions about the role and justification of social institutions more broadly speaking—the subject of theories of justice. If we understand higher education, for example, as an instrument for maximizing social utility overall, then those people with the greatest potential to contribute would be most qualified. It would be unfair to deny access to individuals whose education would serve to maximize social utility, but not necessarily unfair to deny it to others. If higher education is an instrument for maximizing society's economic growth, then restricting access to persons with the best prospects for contributing to maximal economic growth would not be unfair. If our understanding of the proper function of the university is influenced by perfectionist goals of producing excellence, then selecting by criteria that evaluate prospects for excellent achievement would be appropriate. If higher education is shaped by the utopian goal of preparing each person fully to realize his or her potential, then fairness requires that every person should have the opportunity to attend. In each paradigm, fairness requires equal opportunities for those who are suitably qualified.

Fundamental questions about the social function of higher education and hence about the relevant criterion of merit for admission are not easily resolved, especially since universities serve complex roles. I will not attempt to resolve these questions and will address them only in a limited way. I will not, for example, take up the question of whether a greater number of people overall should be entitled to receive a liberal arts education.[13] I will assume, however, that any reasonable conception of fair equality of opportunity will not discriminate by race, gender, or socioeconomic class. The social purpose of the university, however exactly we specify it, should not depend on differential access by race, gender, or class.[14] To this extent, judgments of merit must be constrained by fairness. But since there is no good reason to suspect that raw talent and potential for development and contribution are distributed according to race, gender, or socioeconomic status, this qualification does not distort our common conception of merit.[15] We are free rationally to accept a basic requirement of justice: that qualified and motivated individuals should have equal prospects for attaining positions of social importance, regardless of gender, race, or socioeconomic class of origin. This means that any aggregating and maximizing calculations of the university's value—for instance, attention to the role of the university in promoting a society's economic growth—are objectionable to the extent that they obscure or depend on discrimination by race, gender, or socioeconomic status.

Talent and motivation as criteria of merit might be thought of as useful criteria for correcting historical patterns of discrimination in which some people have attained elite positions by virtue of their social privilege rather than by merit. But talent and motivation as criteria of merit are not easily disaggregated from other factors, because what counts as relevant talent and motivation is socially freighted. Valued aspirations for individuals and institutions are socially conditioned and might be biased, requiring talents and characteristics that reflect the experience and culture of a privileged elite.[16] For example, politicians who are perceived as electable or business leaders who exude authority are more likely to be male, white, and from economically privileged backgrounds. Opportunities to develop talent and motivation are also socially freighted: they are not equally or even randomly distributed but are marked instead by social class, among other factors.[17] We know, for example, that girls are socialized to prefer less quantitative fields of study. We also know that many urban schools fail miserably to prepare students for college. Lack of opportunity is correlated with underdeveloped talent and lower motivation. Natural talent can wither and die.

These challenges raise broader questions of social justice that institutions of higher education have limited means to address. Instead, as I have indicated, my focus is on some possible changes that are within the purview of institutions of higher education to effect.[18] Thus, I acknowledge but do not fully address hard questions about the bearing of gender, race, and socioeconomic class on opportunities to develop talent and motivation as well as on relevant measures of talent, as important as those questions are. Instead, I have chosen to focus on the ethical imperative of achieving greater inclusivity along lines of race, gender, and socioeconomic status according to roughly current appraisals of talent and motivation, including grades and test scores. I do this with some caution and qualification. While I urge broadening current criteria and how we think about them, I do not strongly repudiate current attention to grades and test scores.

The aim of inclusion fits with the self-conscious mission of many colleges and universities. I am speaking here not only of those universities and colleges that embrace affirmative action policies, but also of those whose aim it is to cultivate democratic values, ethical reasoning, critical thinking, and multicultural education. A sampling of liberal arts institutions from around the country bears this out. Terms such as "diversity," "inclusion," and "multiculturalism" are prevalent in the mission statements of many schools. For example, in its mission statement, Yale University states, "Yale seeks to attract a diverse group of exceptionally talented men and women from across the nation and around the world and to educate them for leadership in scholarship, the professions, and society."[19] The mission statement of Colby College includes the goal of providing "a demanding, expansive educational experience to a select group of diverse, talented, intellectually sophisticated students."[20] These themes echo across many American colleges and universities.

Advancing inclusivity by race, gender, and socioeconomic class connects with efforts to remedy historically obvious dimensions of injustice. Underrepresentation is the product of some of the most blatant forms of injustice and is still very much with us today. Addressing other dimensions of injustice will not resolve this problem. The important dimension of corrective and distributive justice is, however, only part of the story I am telling. A genuinely inclusive, deliberative community also models democracy in a participatory sense. Liberal arts colleges and universities are possible sites for the development of an inclusive and deliberative community of equals. The potential for a more inclusive university education to significantly shape the experience and values of its participants also represents its brightest prospects for making a broader social contribution toward greater justice. While higher education is not and is not likely to be universally available, its availability to a substantial segment of the population could be justifiable, provided that segment is diverse and representative.

I am arguing that higher education that is inclusive along the lines of race, gender, and socioeconomic class, and that has a participatory and deliberative orientation, has the potential to shape the values and aims of the members of its community of scholarship to make a valuable civic contribution beyond the university. This rationale for higher education has limits. It does not apply to all institutions of higher learning.[21] Many college students do not receive a deliberative liberal arts education. They attend large lecture classes, they commute to large and diffuse public institutions where they are mostly anonymous, they interrupt their college careers to work (assembling credits over time), and they study vocational fields. Students in these contexts learn not through sustained and deliberative interaction with involved professors and peers, but as relatively passive recipients of information imparted from their professors, at some distance. This model of learning emphasizes formal transfer of knowledge or skills from faculty to individual students. It is modular and not oriented toward community building. Some elements of liberal arts education might be prominent, but without a participatory and deliberative emphasis.

Considerations of distributive and corrective justice provide an argument for fair opportunity to attend institutions of higher education, whether participatory and deliberative or not. I have argued that socially disadvantaged and historically excluded populations should have equal access to important goods conferred by higher education. This imperative of justice could be satisfied by a variety of institutional options, including vocational and technical training as well as large public universities. It does not necessarily require a liberal arts education. The participatory justice argument I have introduced, however, is directed to liberal arts institutions, in particular. If we are to maintain selective liberal arts institutions, rather than, say, utilizing available resources to expand the enrollment capacity of more accessible public institutions, private liberal arts colleges and universities are under moral pressure to reveal unique and valuable contributions whose benefits extend beyond the select class of people who attend these institutions. In other words, the achievements of elite liberal arts institutions should be subjected to ethical evaluation.

I will now elaborate some criteria of ethical evaluation designed to enhance the university as a model of justice. Specifically, I will address student admissions, pedagogy, and the climate on campus for student life and scholarly research. My discussion will be organized by three basic points:

1. Colleges and universities should stress publicly that desert or merit in admissions is best understood as a matter of potential for success and contribution.
2. Scholarship should be evaluated in relation to what I will call "social intelligence."
3. An inclusive and fair campus climate anchors the prospects for critical thinking and creative understanding.

V

The scales of justice are a familiar metaphor for a concept of desert. Desert so understood involves the moral notion that praiseworthy achievers should be rewarded (and, symmetrically, blameworthy wrongdoers should be punished). In this way of thinking, an assessment of past behavior fixes the relevant reward, apart from the implications of past behavior for future performance and from any beneficial consequences that may flow from conferring the award. Furthermore, achievers are thought to be morally entitled to their just deserts. Failure to receive their due would be cause for moral complaint. This notion of desert is backward looking; individual moral desert is fixed without reference to consequences.

Desert is not plausible as an admissions criterion. Admissions committees are charged with identifying persons who will benefit greatly from the school's resources, who will succeed academically, and who will contribute to the school's academic and social mission. Admissions officers look for candidates who merit admission in this complex, forward-looking sense.[22] Grades and standardized test scores are used to predict success rather than serving as achievement indicators of deserved rewards. There is confusion, however, and even resentment in the broader public's perception of judgments of merit in admission. Legal cases have been built on the view that

admitting applicants with lower grades and test scores than their competitors is evidence of unfair treatment, in view of the plaintiffs' superior
achievements, even when universities make it clear that the admissions criteria used further the school's mission in important ways. The U.S. Supreme
Court has not been unsympathetic to the argument that affirmative action
by race is racial discrimination, although it has also not fully accepted the
plaintiffs' arguments, leaving room for admissions criteria to be designed
around merit as individual potential for successful engagement in the collective educational enterprise.[23] It is likely that the court's ambivalence on the
consideration of race in university admissions has fueled public suspicion
of university admissions policies.

Universities with progressive admissions policies should maintain their
stance and communicate it more fully to the public, making clear that diversity is critically important to the collective learning environment. Inclusion
and balance by race, gender, and socioeconomic status promotes the critical-
thinking enterprise, since critical scrutiny of values, biases, and assumptions
is facilitated by thoughtful encounters with people who have had different
social experiences. It should also be stressed that racial diversity and the
inclusion of American minority groups is especially important, given the
profound impact of race on American history, politics, culture, social strati-
fication, and social dynamics.[24] In this respect, the demands of corrective
and distributive justice to remedy disadvantages to historically excluded and
mistreated minorities also promote the collective and individual advancement of learning.

Universities can also communicate more forcefully than they have that
diversification of a student body is best accomplished by limiting the role
of grades and test scores in admissions decisions. Grades and test scores
serve a helpful threshold function for assessing whether a candidate merits
admission, provided that relevant adjustments are made in view of evidence
indicating that certain groups tend to underperform on standardized tests.[25]
However, it should be stressed that candidates also merit admission based
on other factors of practical intelligence, such as ability to overcome obstacles, strength of motivation, commitment, and resilience, as well as the
contribution their individual and cultural perspectives could make to the
learning community. These factors do not compete with merit as criteria of
admission. They are themselves measures of merit in the relevant forward-
looking sense because they figure into the prospects of individual and collective success in learning. The point is that the relevant notion of desert
encompasses potential, it has individual and collective dimensions, and it
is not a moral measure of deserved rewards. While many admissions offices

may affirm this approach, its ethical substance and importance warrants public clarification and emphasis.

Grades and test scores as measures of qualification reveal imbalance by socioeconomic class of origin in the population of students attending elite colleges and universities. Amy Gutmann emphasizes what she refers to as the "big squeeze" in college admissions. In a recent study, Gutmann found that 36 percent of high school seniors who are highly qualified for admission to elite colleges and universities (they have high grades and combined SAT scores over 1200) come from the top 20 percent of the income bracket, while 57 percent of selective university students come from this same income bracket. This means, she concludes, that the "wealthiest 20 percent of American families are overrepresented on elite college campuses by a margin of 21 percent."[26] Gutmann documents underrepresentation of the other income groups all the way down to the lowest income bracket. She found that inadequate financial aid was not the only factor contributing to the underenrollment of qualified students from middle- and lower-income brackets. Also important is the perception that elite universities are unwelcoming. Outreach and retention programs, in addition to need-blind admissions, are crucial to correcting uneven socioeconomic representation of qualified students.

VI

I now turn to the evaluation of scholarship. I propose that scholarship be evaluated for its production of knowledge as "social intelligence." In referring to knowledge as social intelligence, I mean that knowledge can be understood and evaluated in relation to the community of knowers that it empowers. To understand knowledge in relation to social intelligence is to think about how knowledge is built and with whom it is shared. It is to examine who the knowers are, who produces knowledge, and who the intended audience is of knowledge production. The intelligent social group includes those persons who generate and/or can manipulate and expand knowledge. This is the group that renders information useful or in other ways valuable. It might be considerably smaller than the group of people that benefits from the generation of knowledge. Many people benefit from the engineering expertise involved in designing bridges and airplanes, yet few know anything about the principles of engineering and current innovations in the field. At issue here is not the wider social value of advances in research, but rather membership in the intellectual community. The intelligent social group has access to knowledge and can influence its consumption, application, and development, and it has social power that passive beneficiaries lack. Concern with fair opportunity in higher education must address the academic community surrounding scholarship and evaluate its inclusiveness. Fair-opportunity considerations should extend to membership in the community of scholarship.

Institutions involved in education should be concerned with whether the group of people involved with the production and consumption of scholarship is socially representative along lines of race, gender, and social class, and whether students and research faculty at the university are all in a position fully to participate in the scholarship community. This would be to understand social intelligence as the model of deliberative democracy, as opposed to a notion of democracy that emphasizes representation. Consider two differing ideas of political equality. One is that political equality of persons means that the interests of all persons should be given equal weight in collective decisions. This fits with a notion of democracy as representative. The other is the idea that political equality requires equal opportunity to participate in collective decisions.[27] This includes a deliberative requirement. Evaluating knowledge in relation to social intelligence expresses the value of people's opportunities to participate in collective endeavors that affect their basic interests. This expresses a deeper notion of democracy as self-government. It requires more than the production of knowledge as socially beneficial.

I am suggesting that a notion of social intelligence on the model of deliberative democracy be used to evaluate scholarship. Specifically, I am applying it to the community of scholarship and aiming to broaden the social intelligence of scholarship as it bears on the content and conduct of research. If academic departments and, more broadly, academic disciplines are not diversified by race and gender, they should be required by university leadership to broaden their content by opening up new lines of research and/or by hiring women and minorities who are productive scholars, whether or not their subjects of research are race and gender focused. Here I am acknowledging a distinction between race and gender as it bears on the subject of research and the race and gender of researchers themselves. I will count both types of diversification—by topic and by researcher—as progress in terms of race and gender inclusiveness. Inclusiveness by topic potentially calls attention to the nature and sources of justice concerns, increasing our ethical sensitivity. This may facilitate change, if indirectly.

Emphasizing the importance of greater inclusivity does not necessarily imply that there is something wrong with specialized scholarship whose focus is not race and gender. Diversity can be achieved more broadly in academic departments, by hiring minorities and women in those or other areas and also by including areas of scholarship that do study the dynamics of race and gender. Yet subfields that create a chilly climate for women and minorities call for scrutiny, particularly if they lack practical application. Insistence on knowledge for its own sake is troubling when proponents wield scarce resources without inclusive assessment of its promise.

Another strategy for promoting greater inclusiveness emphasizes the value of cross-disciplinary lines of research and centers of scholarship that are designed around inclusive academic research programs, with an eye to cross-fertilizing more recalcitrant fields of study. For example, in "cluster hires" faculty positions are offered to select departments that agree to participate in the curricular development and research advancement of interdisciplinary fields of study. An interdisciplinary committee participates in the selection of candidates for those positions.

Access to the community of scholarship, I have argued, is ideally regulated by a notion of fair equality of opportunity that privileges talent and motivation as qualifications for membership in the community of scholarship and should not otherwise discriminate. Developing the ideal of deliberative democracy in this context contrasts with proposing a broader, society-wide notion of democratic participation that could imply a more radical shift in our thinking about the aims of higher education. Still, applying the idea more narrowly within an understanding of equal opportunity that is structured by the importance of talent and motivation has significant implications for the meaning of equality and inclusion within the academic community. It means that we should be vigilant about whether that community makes up a healthy cross-section by race, gender, and socioeconomic class, as we should expect it would were objectionable bias to be eliminated.

VII

Finally, I turn to some matters of campus climate for students and address the ethics of pedagogy. The phrase "critical thinking" has become popular in descriptions of what university education should aim to cultivate in students.[28] It is not, however, always clear what is meant by the term. In aiming to articulate a plausible understanding, let us first distinguish between passive and active thought. In passive thinking students absorb information but do not consciously identify reasons to endorse or to reject the value of this information. Memorization and regurgitation of information are examples of passive thinking. Active, critical thinking, by contrast, survives reflective endorsement. It involves judgment and evaluation and is guided by values.[29]

In reflectively endorsing the relevance of information, a person's self-conception and values are used as guides for appraising information and orienting the quest for knowledge.[30] Values enable a person to explore new information by placing him or her in a position to evaluate whether information is worthy of consideration. In thinking critically, one has a sense of the point of exploring information. For example, it might serve a potentially valuable social purpose, sharpen our understanding and appreciation of the natural world, or be emotionally and intellectually satisfying. Because a framework of values places a person in a position to recognize information as providing reasons for further thought and for drawing conclusions, critical thinking is connected with self-affirmation. It involves coming to conclusions by means of reasons that one affirms as relevant. When a person adopts reasons as a basis for drawing conclusions, he or she may become aware that they say something about who he or she is. The person is one who has certain aims in the thinking enterprise that he or she believes makes it worthwhile. To avoid cognitive dissonance, we put ourselves under some pressure to see that the reasons we recognize fit together, if not into one overall rational scheme, then at least into rational clusters, eliminating obvious conflicts. We have a stake in seeing that these clusters cohere, more or less, over time so that we can experience ourselves as unified persons.

Critical thinking, as I have just described it, is an exercise in autonomy. By autonomy, however, I do not mean isolation. In fact, critical thinking as an exercise in autonomy typically requires social presence. It requires that other people affirm the integrity of one's intellectual capacities. Without relevant social acknowledgment it is very difficult for people to use critical thinking to learn new things. This is because in thinking critically one reaches out from what one understands and thinks is important to explore new information and ideas and also to reflect on one's assumptions and commitments. Critical thinking begins from and is oriented by a person's values and reasons, but it also involves scrutinizing the values and reasons upon which a person's identity depends. Thus it involves self-evaluation. This requires constructive modes of challenge that can facilitate individual self-evaluation. A diverse community with a collective commitment to honest and open inquiry is an invaluable tool for critical thinking and learning.

Thinking critically together with other people introduces an ethical dimension. A process of self-examination can be difficult and even painful. One might discover that some of one's values, assumptions, and commitments do not have the support of reason—they cannot be justified or do not, on reflection, seem worthwhile. Students who are open to learning sometimes discover this. Critical thinking as an exercise in self-reflection can provoke a palpable sense of vulnerability and disorientation; social support may be needed to enable the critical-thinking exercise to continue. Educators thus have a complex role: as supporters and as guides who introduce worthwhile sources of challenge and promote collective reasoning that satisfies ethical requirements of mutual respect.[31] Teaching a diverse group of students complicates the responsibilities involved in teaching. The starting point for critical thinking differs across people, particularly in a diverse group in which different people have different life experiences and values. Educators must develop multiple strategies for engaging students. This suggests a certain ethics of teaching—emphasizing that instructors should not only model active, engaged learning, but should also use multiple and varied representations of course content and incorporate student-centered teaching (such as dialogue, informal writing, group discussion, team projects, and other forms of cooperative learning).

When critical thinking is a genuinely collective enterprise, all participants must be recognized as capable of rational judgment and honest self-evaluation. Each will be treated as capable of gaining knowledge and evaluating information in good faith. This means that participants are under ethical pressure to recognize one another as capable of challenging, scrutinizing, and evaluating the bases of knowledge claims. They must recognize one another as worthy interlocutors. One is thus challenged to broaden one's self-assessment to rationally engage the perspective of other people, although their starting points may be quite different from one's own. Accepting this challenge expresses ethical respect for the autonomy of other people and enables mutual and collective growth.

Evidence from social psychology supports my proposal that we understand critical thinking as an exercise in autonomy that depends on ethical group dynamics. Studies confirm, for example, that threats to self-esteem (e.g., stereotype threat), cultural alienation, and the perception of bias and unfairness significantly affect the academic performance of women and students of color.[32] Fair and socially affirmative responses to these threats have been shown to improve student performance significantly.[33] This is evidence in favor of an ethics of pedagogy that is student centered, participatory, and sensitive to the importance and difficulty of creating group dynamics that engender mutual respect and equal standing.

VIII

This essay has attempted to give content to the idea of the university as a model of justice in meeting reasonable institutional requirements of justice that address historically rooted sources of exclusion, and in promoting an inclusive culture in the academic community, on the model of the university community as a participatory democracy. I have argued that this realizable ideal of the university encompasses the university's approach to admissions, scholarship, campus climate, and pedagogy. Inclusivity in these aspects of a university's policies and mission is required as a matter of fair equality of opportunity, and it is critical to developing the potential of liberal arts education to enhance critical thinking, ethical reasoning, and democratic values. Were universities successfully to model justice in the ways I have described, faculty and students broadly representative of the wider population and enabled fully to participate in the learning and research community would be in a strong position to represent their own experiences and to shape the values of the institution. By influencing their peers as well as developing personally, all members of the academic community could influence the social role and contribution of the university. This would raise the prospects for universities justly to contribute to the broader social good, rather than merely serving the interests of a privileged population.

Notes

I would like to thank Paula Frederick for research assistance and comments on this essay. For valuable comments and discussion I am grateful to Peter Levine, Harry Brighouse, Lionel McPherson, Michael McPherson, Julio Garcia, Steven Macedo, and participants in a Spencer Foundation workshop (June 2011) and conference (Northwestern University, October 2011) on the aims of higher education.

1. See Martha Nussbaum, *Not for Profit: Why Democracy Needs the Humanities* (Princeton, NJ: Princeton University Press, 2010).
2. See Jürgen Habermas, "Discourse Ethics: Notes on a Program of Philosophical Justification," in *Moral Consciousness and Communicative Action*, trans. Christian Lenhardt and Shierry Weber Nicholsen, introd. Thomas McCarthy (Cambridge, MA: The MIT Press, 1990).
3. See Eamonn Callan, *Creating Citizens* (Oxford: Oxford University Press, 1997).
4. This theme is prominent in Amy Gutmann's essay "What Makes a University Education Worthwhile?," this volume.
5. While broad-based assessment tools are important for all educational institutions, learning outcomes in liberal arts institutions might be especially challenging to measure.
6. By "liberal," I mean a society that protects equal basic rights, fair opportunities, and a decent standard of living for all.
7. Oberlin College and Berea College are examples of institutions with a history of strong commitment to racial diversity. That is admirable, yet those institutions have not achieved full commitment to modeling justice as I describe it.
8. See *Engines of Economic Growth: The Economic Impact of Boston's Eight Research Universi-*

ties on the Metropolitan Boston Area (New York: Appleseed, 2003); www.appleseedinc
.com/reports/Boston_summary.pdf (accessed August 28, 2014).

9. For a helpful and more detailed development of similar lines of criticism, see Christopher Bertram, "Defending the Humanities in a Liberal Society," this volume. Bertram raises concerns about the environmental effects of consumption, among other concerns.

10. For discussion of problems with the business model, see Peter Katopes, "The 'Business Model' Is the Wrong Model," *Inside Higher Ed*, September 20, 2011, http://www
.insidehighered.com/views/2009/02/16/katopes (accessed August 28, 2014).

11. For a discussion of this type of model and its effect on the preparation of students to participate in a diverse democracy, see Barry Checkoway, "Renewing the Civic Mission of the American Research University," *Journal of Higher Education* 72, no. 2 (March–April 2001): 125–47.

12. This argument does not depend on whether institutions of higher education succeed in promoting a democratic and egalitarian political culture in the broader society.

13. It might be argued that institutions of higher education should be expanded so that more people have an opportunity to attend. Alternatively, merit as a criterion for admission could be jettisoned and replaced by open enrollment or a lottery system. This takes us back to questions about the value of higher education, and whether this value has (or ought to have) strong enough public support to prioritize equal chances or universal access as a matter of justice.

14. This claim is not in tension with affirmative action policies, which aim to correct historically entrenched patterns of discrimination.

15. Despite a long history of gender discrimination, many selective colleges (although not in the Ivy League) now have more female than male students, reflecting qualifications gained prior to college and perhaps also reasonable judgments about potential. This raises some serious questions about whether primary and secondary school education is failing adequately to serve boys. Thanks to Harry Brighouse for calling this issue to my attention.

16. See, e.g., discussions of cultural bias in standardized testing.

17. Greg J. Duncan and Richard Murnane, eds., *Whither Opportunity? Rising Inequality, Schools, and Children's Life Chances* (New York: Russell Sage Foundation, and Chicago: Spencer Foundation, 2011); J. Brooks-Gunn and F. F. Furstenberg, "The Children of Adolescent Mothers: Academic and Psychological Outcomes," *Developmental Review* 6 (1986): 224–51; Todd R. Risley and Betty Hart, *Meaningful Differences in the Everyday Experience of Young American Children* (Baltimore, MD: Paul H. Brookes, 1995); Edmund W. Gordon and Melissa P. Lemons, "An Interactionist Perspective on the Genesis of Intelligence," in *Intelligence, Heredity, and Environment*, ed. Robert J. Sternberg and Elena Grigorenko (New York: Cambridge University Press, 1997), 323–40.

18. For discussion of the responsibility of universities to address racial inequalities in pre-college education, see Lionel K. McPherson, "Righting Injustice in Higher Education," this volume.

19. http://www.yale.edu/about/mission.html.

20. See http://www.colby.edu/academics_cs/catalogue/2011_2012/general_information /colby_plan.cfm (accessed August 28, 2014). See also the mission statements for the following schools: Colgate College http://colgate.edu/about/generalinformation /mission/html, the University of Washington (http://www.washington.edu/diversity/), the University of North Dakota (http://und.edu/discover/leadership-and-educators

/mission-statement. cfm), and Grinnell College (http://www.grinnell.edu/offices
/president/ missionstatement), to name a few.

21. Thanks to Peter Levine for his suggestions on this paragraph.

22. This is something like the notion of desert that David Schmidtz refers to as a promis-
sory notion. See David Schmidtz, *Elements of Justice* (Cambridge: Cambridge University Press, 2006), chapter 8.

23. See *Grutter v. Bollinger* 539 U.S. 306 (2003). See also *Regents of the University of California v. Bakke* 438 U.S. 265 (1978). The Supreme Court is currently considering a
challenge to the consideration of race in university admissions: *Fisher v. University of
Texas at Austin*, No. 11–345 (2012).

24. This argument appears to be absent from the respondents' arguments to the court in
Fisher v. University of Texas at Austin. The respondents argue for the educational benefits of diversity without emphasizing the central importance to American society of
the dynamics and social history of race. They do not go beyond the stance taken by
the petitioners in *Regents of the University of California v. Bakke*.

25. See Christopher Jencks and Meredith Phillips, *The Black-White Test Score Gap* (Washington, DC: Brookings Institution Press, 1998); and Richard E. Nisbett, *Intelligence
and How to Get It: Why Schools and Cultures Count* (New York: W. W. Norton, 2009).

26. Amy Gutmann, "What Makes a University Education Worthwhile?," this volume.

27. See Joshua Cohen, "Procedure and Substance in Deliberative Democracy," in *Philosophy, Politics, Democracy: Selected Essays* (Cambridge, MA: Harvard University Press,
2009). See also Ronald Dworkin, "The Curse of American Politics," *New York Review
of Books*, October 17, 1996.

28. I am not supposing that a liberal arts education is the only way to cultivate critical
thinking.

29. For a thoughtful discussion of values associated with critical thinking, see Kyla Ebels-
Duggan, "Autonomy as Intellectual Virtue," this volume.

30. See Christine M. Korsgaard, *The Sources of Normativity*, ed. Onora O'Neill (Cambridge:
Cambridge University Press, 1996), especially chapter 3, and *Self-Constitution: Agency,
Identity, and Integrity* (Oxford: Oxford University Press, 2009), chapter 1.

31. See Paul Weithman's thoughtful discussion in this volume on the importance of
teachers as academic friends. In their contributions to this volume, both Weithman
and Ebels-Duggan stress the importance of teachers' demonstrating love for the ideas
they teach and admiration for the tenacity needed for developing complex ideas.
Their discussions helpfully counter a tendency in some approaches to critical thinking of a negative debate-style emphasis on the vulnerability of complex positions to
objections.

32. See Claude M. Steele, *Whistling Vivaldi and Other Clues to How Stereotypes Affect Us*
(New York: W. W. Norton, 2010); Geoffrey L. Cohen and Claude M. Steele, "A Barrier
of Mistrust: How Negative Stereotypes Affect Cross-Race Mentoring," in *Improving
Academic Achievement: Impact of Psychological Factors on Education*," ed. J. Aronson
(San Diego, CA: Academic Press, 2002); Yen J. Huo, Heather J. Smith, Tom R. Tyler,
and E. Allan Lind, "Superordinate Identification, Subgroup Identification, and Jus-
tice Concerns: Is Separatism the Problem, Is Assimilation the Answer?," *Psychological
Science* 7, no. 1 (1996): 40–45; Albert Bandura, *Social Foundations of Thought and
Action: A Social Cognitive Theory* (Englewood Cliffs, NJ: Prentice-Hall, 1986); and
Carol S. Dweck, *Self-Theories: Their Role in Motivation, Personality, and Development*
(Philadelphia: Taylor & Francis/Psychology Press, 1999).

33. G. L. Cohen, J. Garcia, N. Apfel, and A. Master, "Reducing the Racial Achievement

Gap: A Social-Psychological Intervention," *Science* 313 (2006), 1307–10; and G. L. Cohen, J. Garcia, V. Purdie-Vaugns, N. Apfel, and P. Brzustoski, "Recursive Processes in Self-Affirmation: Intervening to Close the Minority Achievement Gap," *Science* 324 (2009): 400–403. Even seemingly small interventions have been shown to have a significant impact. See T. D. Wilson, "The Power of Social-Psychological Interventions," *Science* 313 (2006): 1251–52; and Julio Garcia and Geoffrey L. Cohen, "A Social Psychological Approach to Educational Intervention," in *The Behavioral Foundations of Policy*, ed. Eldar Shafir (Princeton, NJ: Princeton University Press, 2012).

NINE

Conclusion:
Future Research on Values
in Higher Education

HARRY BRIGHOUSE AND MICHAEL MCPHERSON

Our aim is to get readers to engage with the normative questions in higher education the authors have discussed. But numerous policy and practice issues involve important normative dimensions; no book could reasonably cover them all. In this brief concluding chapter we outline a number of issues about which, we believe, decision making would be improved if informed by careful normative thinking supported by philosophical concepts.

1. Careful philosophical work on the purposes and aims of higher education is sparse.[1] Several contributions to this volume touch on these questions, but clearly more would be valuable. Derek Bok has articulated an ambitious account of the purposes of higher education, which charges college with preparing students to think critically, become good citizens, live well with diversity, become equipped for a career, and be able to act ethically.[2] Stanley Fish counters with an extremely narrow account, in which the only purpose is to present students with an invitation to our academic disciplines.[3] Anthony Kronman offers a third, equally narrow alternative: that the purpose of higher education is to provide students with the resources to explore the meanings of their lives and discover who they really are.[4] All three accounts merit careful philosophical scrutiny, which they have not so far received. This debate matters greatly to administrators deciding where to put their marginal resources. Should they, for example, fund additional student services, or additional faculty? If they add student services, which are most important? If they opt for more faculty, on what grounds should they choose among departments? Should they add academic staff rather than tenure lines? The debate also matters to decisions about how to structure programs.

For example, should professional development focus on instructional improvement, curriculum development, or, for that matter, development of counseling skills in faculty members?

2. The purposes of higher education have implications for how professors and other teachers should think of their jobs—what their job description should be. Says Fish:

> I am trained and paid to do two things (although, needless to say, I don't always succeed in my attempts to do them): (1) to introduce students to materials they didn't know a whole lot about, and (2) to equip them with the skills that will enable them, first, to analyze and evaluate those materials and, second, to perform independent research, should they choose to do so, after the semester is over. That's it. That's the job. There's nothing more.[5]

This seems right if his narrow conception of the purpose of higher education is correct; but on the more comprehensive conception Bok offers, it seems plausible that the professor has a more complex job description. He or she should not only prompt academic learning in the students, but should be alert, and prepared, to provide guidance in meeting some of their needs that are not directly academic. Perhaps professors should be trained in basic counseling techniques: how to craft emails to students who are skipping class, how to approach students who seem to be withdrawn or depressed, and how to distinguish students who merely seem withdrawn and depressed from those who actually are. It is certainly true, as Fish observes, that people who are currently professors are not selected for the characteristics that predict good performance of a job involving these judgments: "I can't speak for every college teacher, but I'm neither trained nor paid to do any of those things, although I am aware of people who are: ministers, therapists, social workers, political activists, gurus, inspirational speakers and diversity consultants."[6] Perhaps we should select different kinds of people for the job or embrace an explicit division of labor among the faculty, in which some specialize more in research and others in teaching, success in which for a diverse student body requires sensitivity and skills that Fish says he lacks.

3. In loco parentis, the doctrine that colleges had strong paternalistic authority over students' personal behavior, has long been abandoned on most campuses, but in the past thirty years student services designed to support students who lack other sources of guidance, or for whom those other sources are inadequate, have proliferated on most selective campuses. Christian

Smith's study of emerging adults, *Lost in Transition*,[7] is just one of a number
of studies suggesting that college-age youths find the transition to adulthood difficult to navigate without help; his study documents confusion,
often self-destructive, about drugs and alcohol, sex, consumer society, and
political activity. This literature, especially when combined with the more
ambitious accounts of the purposes of higher education, suggests that some
careful philosophical examination of the doctrine of in loco parentis, and
the reasons for and against reinstating some modified version of it, might be
in order.

4. The rise of online learning poses a number of challenges to administrators
    and the sector as a whole. Some of these challenges might be navigated bet-
    ter with the help of philosophical work. Here we outline just three of these
    challenges:

    a. Online learning raises the question of who (morally) owns the con-
        tent of a course. Traditionally professors have regarded themselves,
        and been treated as, owners of the curricular materials they design,
        the lectures they give, the discussion prompts and assessments they
        use, and most of the other intellectual materials associated with
        teaching. Traditionally, a lecture was ephemeral; after it was given, it
        no longer existed. Now a lecture can be captured and placed online
        as part of a course. When the professor moves to another college or
        ceases to teach that course, does the college for which he gave it have
        an obligation to compensate him for continuing to use the video?
        Is he morally permitted to take the materials, including the videos,
        with him for his new employer to use? What about the other course
        materials he has developed and placed online? If the answers are that
        the materials belong to the institution that paid his salary while he
        was developing them, and on whose students he tested the materials,
        then why is the same not true (if it is not) of textbooks, which tradi-
        tionally authors have claimed as their intellectual property, but from
        which their employers have not derived an income?

    b. Online learning enables institutions to monitor the teaching pro-
        cess much more easily and cheaply than they can with in-classroom
        teaching. This, in turn, enables them to preempt the judgment of
        teachers and enforce standardized curriculums and even instruction.
        In 2012 officials at San Jose State University suggested that its phi-
        losophy department teach an applied ethics course using Harvard
        professor Michael Sandel's free online lectures as part of the course.
        During the ensuing discussion, some suggested that faculty mem-
        bers have a right to determine the content of their own courses. Do

they, in fact, have that right? Do they, as some faculty think, have rights over the manner of delivery of their courses? Should a tenured professor be entitled to refuse to teach in an online or blended environment? College practices are in flux, and regulations are being shaped over the coming years. Organizational knowledge and an understanding of the law and of the economics of the new environment are key to getting things right, but careful normative thought about what moral rights professors have to autonomy in the design and delivery of courses is also needed in order for college leaders to forge better practices and regulations.

c. Online learning promises to enable us to educate students more efficiently by lowering costs. Some experimental evidence suggests that impressive gains in the teaching of calculus and other technical subjects are attainable. But college does not only provide students with technical academic skills. Attending a residential college—or just spending a good deal of time in a classroom—with other students who are unlike them in various ways enables them to learn different ways of engaging with other people. Additionally, students from relatively disadvantaged home and educational backgrounds can learn some of the habits and practices that support success in professional life. As Jennifer Morton comments, for many students from disadvantaged backgrounds, college is where for the first time "they have spoken in front of a crowd of students from differing socioeconomic and ethnic backgrounds. The experience is terrifying, but as one Latina student told me, even though her face still 'lights up red' when she speaks, she is now able to raise her hand and contribute to class discussions. By the time that student graduates and walks into her first job interview, she will have learned to manage her fear of speaking her mind."[8] Whereas relatively advantaged students may, for some time to come, attend residential face-to-face colleges, because of the prestige and networking opportunities they create and the fact that for their parents costs are not a large problem, the students whose education is most likely to migrate online are those for whom cost is an issue, but who are most in need of the benefits that a residential college can provide. Could judiciously designed online environments replicate these learning opportunities? If not, or if not for some time, how should decision makers weigh the cost savings against the potential costs to disadvantaged students? Experience and research have yet to show us exactly what can and cannot be achieved through online teaching. Moral philosophizing is needed to tell us what we should be looking for: what differences between online and face-to-face environments we should be looking for, and what tradeoffs we should be willing or unwilling to make.

5. Higher education is subsidized by the states and the federal government, and it is easy to see the moral questions about why states should give subsidies to those who have benefited most from the K–12 system but not to those whom that system has benefited least. But states are not the only subsidizers of education. Selective colleges use endowment money to subsidize students and tuition policies to cross-subsidize. Subsidized students include those from low-income or other disadvantaged backgrounds. They also include students with very high prior academic achievement, as well as athletes (including the large majority of college athletes, whose activities produce no revenues) and students who take high-cost majors. Some colleges charge a small premium for high-cost majors whose graduates can expect higher than average earnings (such as business and engineering) but few charge extra for high-cost majors with low expected earnings, such as music, art, or drama. Flagship state universities vary a great deal in their tuition policies: some adopt a high-tuition/high-aid model for resident students, while others hold to a low-tuition/low-aid policy. Careful philosophical work that helps decision makers identify and properly weigh the complex moral issues raised by different aspects of tuition and aid policy will have to attend carefully to empirical details, but in our view it is much needed.

6. We have mentioned athletes as recipients of subsidies. In fact, preferences and subsidies for athletes in selective U.S. colleges and universities on average benefit students who are more economically advantaged than average. But it is not clear whether we should really describe tuition remission and grants for athletes in revenue-generating sports as subsidies. Owing to the arrangements between the NFL and NBA on one side, and the NCAA on the other, aspiring football and basketball players are all but forced to offer their services to a college for some period of time. They are offered scholarships and a college education, but the conditions under which they are forced to work for the scholarships—which involve extensive travel, intensive training, and seclusion into a peer group with low academic aspirations—make it impossible for most to take full advantage of that education. The compensation for many of the best athletes in these sports is nowhere close to what their market wage would be absent this restrictive practice, and will continue to be so even when the recent court ruling requiring the NCAA to allow players to receive up to $5,000 per year comes into effect in 2016. Philosophical work scrutinizing the justifiability of these arrangements would be welcome.

7. Much attention has been given to the question of whether it is legitimate or perhaps even morally required for colleges to give preferences to racial minorities in the admissions process. Much less attention has been given to other pervasive kinds of preference—for example, preferences that result in geographic diversity. Although there has been work on affirmative action for women, that has tended to focus on affirmative action as correcting for ambition-stunting, or discriminatory, behavior of families and schools. No attention, as far as we know, has been given to a new form of affirmative action: affirmative action for boys. The academic gender gap, which once favored boys, now favors girls, and without any readily discernible cause rooted in discrimination or attempts to stunt ambition. Whereas the social consequences of the racial achievement gap are clear, and the social consequences of the gender achievement gap when it favored boys were clear, the social consequences of this new gap are unknown. Should colleges practice affirmative action for boys, who are not a historically disadvantaged group? If so, why, and in what ways?

8. Professors have a good deal of choice about what to research and how to divide their time between teaching, research, and service. Tenure protects this choice, but as with many other areas of one's personal and professional life, being free to choose does not absolve one from the moral consequences of one's choices. Some topics for research are more socially valuable than others. It is hard to believe, for example, that the probable marginal social benefit of a new essay on the portrayal of tea drinking in the Victorian novel is the same as that of a new study of the effects of teaching Victorian literature in a particular way to eleventh-graders, or adding a voluntary discussion section for secondary-education English majors to one's Victorian literature class. The literature scholar, of course, has a specific skill set, but that skill set is not fixed; he or she can learn new research methods that may be better suited to investigating more socially pressing issues, or new ways of teaching Victorian literature to prospective or current high school English teachers. We are not suggesting that there is no place for pure research, nor even that universities should exert control over the research choices of faculty; we are merely observing that there is a neglected moral issue here concerning which philosophical work might be helpful. Academia is a profession without a well-articulated professional ethic. Professors understand that they should not sleep with their students, plagiarize, fake results, or criticize their colleagues' teaching (not necessarily in that order), but as ethics go this is pretty thin. The professional development of professors rarely attends closely to decision making about time and effort allocation; similarly, the literature on the ethics of individual time allocation is sparse.

9. Questions of value very obviously infuse the teaching and study of the humanities and, perhaps less obviously, are deeply implicated in the teaching and study of the social sciences. Because moral and political philosophers, and philosophers of education, frequently teach students about contemporary moral controversies, it is surprising and disappointing that literature on the ethics of teaching about questions of value in college is so sparse. What criteria should professors use when selecting topics within a course? Should they disclose their own views about the issues at hand, and should the answer to that question depend on how well they can get to know their students? What should their learning objectives be for the students, and should those objectives vary depending on the students' major and whether they are taking the course as an elective or requirement? When an election looms and in-class discussion is either unavoidable or desirable, should the professor disclose his or her voting intentions?[9]

We do not want to take a stand on any of the questions that we have identified above, although we suspect that our framing of some of them gives away our intuitive judgments. But we hope that readers will feel emboldened to consider, and ideally to pursue, some of these questions in order to enrich philosophical—and ultimately, we hope, professional and public—discourse about higher education.

Notes

1. We invited Amy Gutmann to contribute for several reasons, but one was that she is that rare practicing political philosopher who has written in some detail about the aims of higher education, in *Democratic Education* (Princeton, NJ: Princeton University Press, 1989).
2. Derek Bok, *Our Underachieving Colleges: A Candid Look at How Much Students Learn and Why They Should Be Learning More* (Princeton, NJ: Princeton University Press, 1989).
3. Stanley Fish, *Save the World on Your Own Time* (New York: Oxford University Press, 2008).
4. Anthony Kronman, *Education's End: Why Our Colleges and Universities Have Given Up on the Meaning of Life* (New Haven, CT: Yale University Press, 2008).
5. Stanley Fish, "Tip to Professors: Just Do Your Job," *New York Times*, October 22, 2006, http://opinionator.blogs.nytimes.com/2006/10/22/tip-to-professors-just-do-your-job/?_php=true&_type=blogs&_r=0 (accessed. August 28, 2014).
6. Ibid.
7. Christian Smith, *Lost in Transition: The Dark Side of Emerging Adulthood* (Notre Dame, IN: University of Notre Dame Press, 2011).
8. Jennifer Morton, "Unequal Classrooms: What Online Education Cannot Teach," *Chronicle of Higher Education* blog, July 29, 2013, http://chronicle.com/blogs

/conversation/2013/07/29/unequal-classrooms-what-online-education-cannot
-teach/ (accessed August 28, 2014).

9. For valuable discussions of these issues as they arise in secondary school teaching, see Diana E. Hess, *Controversy in the Classroom: The Democratic Power of Discussion* (New York: Routledge, 2008); and Diana E. Hess and Paula McAvoy, *The Political Classroom: Evidence and Ethics in Democratic Education* (New York: Routledge, 2014).

ACKNOWLEDGMENTS

The editors feel very fortunate to have had the help of so many capable people in the preparation of this volume. A variety of tasks necessary to developing and editing this volume were performed by Spencer Foundation staff, including, most prominently, Doris Fischer and Judy Klippenstein from the outset and Raymonda Reese and Gladys Reyes in the late stages. Elizabeth Branch Dyson at the University of Chicago Press was a constant source of support and well-judged advice. The authors and editors are grateful for valuable advice and criticism to Jaime Ahlberg, Richard Arneson, Derek Bok, Ann Cudd, Diana Hess, David Hilbert, Morty Schapiro, Seana Shiffrin, and Laurie Zoloth.

CONTRIBUTORS

CHRISTOPHER BERTRAM is Professor of Social and Political Philosophy at the Department of Philosophy, University of Bristol. His main research interests are in theories of justice (especially global distributive justice, including issues concerning territory and migration) and in the thought of Jean-Jacques Rousseau.

HARRY BRIGHOUSE is Professor of Philosophy and Affiliate Professor of Educational Policy Studies at the University of Wisconsin, Madison. His teaching focuses mainly on issues in political philosophy and applied ethics. His most recent book (with Adam Swift) is *Family Values: The Ethics of Parent-Child Relations* (Princeton University Press, 2014). He served for seven years as Senior Program Associate of the Spencer Foundation's Initiative on Philosophy in Educational Policy and Practice with Michael McPherson.

ALLEN BUCHANAN is James B. Duke Professor of Philosophy and Professor of Law at Duke University. He also holds ongoing part-time visiting positions at the University of Arizona and King's College London Law School. His research is mainly in bioethics, political philosophy, and philosophy of international law. His most recent book is *The Heart of Human Rights* (Oxford University Press, 2013).

KYLA EBELS-DUGGAN is Associate Professor of Philosophy at Northwestern University. She works on moral and political philosophy and their history, especially the work of Immanuel Kant. She has published articles in *Philosophical Studies*, *Philosophers' Imprint*, *Ethics*, and the *Philosophical Quarterly*.

AMY GUTMANN, president of the University of Pennsylvania since 2004, is the author or editor of thirteen books, including *Democratic Education* and, most recently, *The Spirit of Compromise* with Dennis Thompson (Princeton University Press, 2012). She is the Christopher H. Browne Distinguished Professor of Political Science and Professor of Communication in the Annenberg School for Communication, with secondary faculty appointments in Philosophy and the Graduate School of Education. Her areas of scholarly expertise include educational policy, deliberation in democracy, bioethics, access to higher education and health care, professional ethics, and ethics and public policy.

ERIN I. KELLY is Associate Professor and Department Chair of Philosophy at Tufts University. Her research interests are in moral and political philosophy and the philosophy of law, with a focus on questions about justice, the nature of moral reasons, moral responsibility and desert, and theories of punishment.

LIONEL K. MCPHERSON is Associate Professor of Philosophy at Tufts University. His publications, which range from ethics to political and social philosophy, include "Normativity and the Rejection of Rationalism" (*Journal of Philosophy*) and "Is Terrorism Distinctively Wrong?" (*Ethics*). He currently is writing a book, *The Afterlife of Race*, about racial identity, political solidarity, and black progress.

MICHAEL MCPHERSON is the fifth President of the Spencer Foundation. Prior to joining the Foundation in 2003, he served as President of Macalester College in St. Paul, Minnesota, for seven years. A nationally known economist whose expertise focuses on the interplay between education and economics, McPherson spent the twenty-two years prior to his Macalester presidency as Professor of Economics, Chairman of the Economics Department, and Dean of Faculty at Williams College in Williamstown, Massachusetts.

PAUL WEITHMAN is the Glynn Family Honors Collegiate Professor of Philosophy at the University of Notre Dame, where he has taught since 1991 and where he has won several awards for his teaching. He is the author of *Religion and the Obligations of Citizenship* (Cambridge University Press, 2000), *Why Political Liberalism?* (Oxford University Press, 2010), and numerous articles in moral philosophy, political philosophy, and the philosophy of education. He is currently a co-director of Notre Dame's Glynn Family Honors Program and the director of its program in Philosophy, Politics and Economics.

INDEX

academic friendship, 5, 52–71, 155n31; autonomy and, 52, 56–61; developing qualities of mind in, 52–54, 66–69; as elite ideal, 52, 69–71; goals of, 52–53; imagination and, 61–62, 66, 71, 72n17; inequalities in, 54–55; investigation of intellectual complexity in, 64–65; limited duration of, 69; sharing of informed appreciation in, 62–63, 68–69; types of relationships in, 52–56
academic gender gap, 162
academy schools, 128–32, 135n46
access to higher education, 4, 8–14, 24n12, 148
Ackerman, Bruce, 89n8
active thought, 150–51. *See also* critical thinking
admissions policies, 5–6; desert and merit in, 146–48; equal opportunity practices in, 115–19, 122, 130, 133n10, 141–46, 162; grades and test scores in, 147–48; need-blind practices in, 12, 24n14. *See also* diversity (demographic)
advancement of knowledge, 28–29, 44–47, 137, 147–50. *See also* investigation of intellectual complexity
advantages of higher education, 1–2
affirmative action, 116–19, 134n33, 154n14; class-conscious policies in, 127–28; diversity rationale in, 123, 125–28; gender achievement gap and, 162; reverse discrimination and, 123, 134n31; US Supreme Court decisions on, 116–18, 126, 155nn23–24

Altschuler, Glenn, 120, 121
Aristotle, 53–56, 84
Arneson, Richard, 49n5, 132n4
arts, the. *See* humanities, the
athletics, 161
Aumann, Robert, 72n17
authority of reason, 5, 57–61; empirical limitations on, 92–94; kinds of rational support in, 57–59, 72n13; modeling of, 59–61, 87; vs. victory in argument, 69
autonomy, 4–5, 74–87; academic friendship and, 52, 56–61; appreciation of positive conviction in, 81, 83, 87; authority of reason in, 57–59, 72n13; charity and humility in, 74, 82–88, 91nn21–23; content neutrality in, 85–86; critical thinking in, 76–77, 80–81, 151; modeling of, 59–61, 87; moral individualism in, 78–79; prescription of fixes for, 74, 76–77, 79–81; prognosis for, 74, 76–77; reconceptualization of, 74–75, 81–87; standard conception of, 74–77, 85–86, 88–89nn7–10; tenacity in, 83–87, 91nn22; threats to, 74–79, 88n4

basketball scholarships, 161
Bate, Jonathan, 50n26
beliefs, 5, 99–101; role of emotion in, 107–10; subversion of moral values and, 101–3, 112n9
Berea College, 153n7
Bertram, Christopher, 4, 72n17, 154n9
Bioethics Commission, 15–16, 24n15